The Creator of
the Wombles

The Creator of the Wombles

The First Biography of Elisabeth Beresford

Kate Robertson

WHITE OWL

AN IMPRINT OF PEN & SWORD BOOKS LTD.
YORKSHIRE - PHILADELPHIA

First published in Great Britain in 2023 by
White Owl
An imprint of Pen & Sword Books Limited
Yorkshire – Philadelphia

Copyright © Kate Robertson 2023

ISBN 978 1 52679 466 6

Typeset by Mac Style
Printed in the UK by CPI Group (UK) Ltd, Croydon, CR0 4YY.

Pen & Sword Books Limited incorporates the imprints of After
the Battle, Atlas, Archaeology, Aviation, Discovery, Family History,
Fiction, History, Maritime, Military, Military Classics, Politics,
Select, Transport, True Crime, Air World, Frontline Publishing, Leo
Cooper, Remember When, Seaforth Publishing, The Praetorian Press,
Wharncliffe Local History, Wharncliffe Transport, Wharncliffe True
Crime and White Owl.

For a complete list of Pen & Sword titles please contact

PEN & SWORD BOOKS LIMITED
47 Church Street, Barnsley, South Yorkshire, S70 2AS, England
E-mail: enquiries@pen-and-sword.co.uk
Website: www.pen-and-sword.co.uk
or
PEN AND SWORD BOOKS
1950 Lawrence Rd, Havertown, PA 19083, USA
E-mail: Uspen-and-sword@casematepublishers.com
Website: www.penandswordbooks.com

For the island of Alderney and her people past, present and future with my love and thanks.

Contents

Introduction

Elisabeth Beresford, known to her friends as Liza, was a compulsive writer. Over a career spanning sixty years, she wrote millions of words for book publishers, magazines, newspapers, theatre, television and radio on the most eclectic range of subjects from lipsticks to literacy. Her driving force was 'to keep the bank balance in the black', because she had a constant fear of debt. Yet when released from the pressures of daily grind, when her imagination was given full rein, she wrote sublime children's fiction which was to culminate in the creation of *The Wombles*.

Liza's life was what she called, 'A series of roller-coaster rides': never dull, often extraordinary, packed with incident, hard work, and financial highs and lows. She was terrified of poverty – with good reason. She was the fourth child and only daughter of a successful but sometimes impecunious author, leading a peripatetic life in France and England; her father left the marital home in 1939 and her redoubtable mother was forced to take in paying guests to make ends meet. There were deprivations in the Second World War and in addition to rationing, her childhood home was bombed twice. In 1949 she married Max Robertson, a BBC sports commentator and television personality whose fortunes fluctuated with the tide; and with two children, her mother, paying guests, a live-in secretary and two domestic staff to manage and support, she was compelled to write for anyone who would pay her.

As a journalist she typed out millions of words on her trusty 'tryper' as my brother Marcus and I called her portable Olivetti typewriter; on radio she interviewed people from all walks of life, but it was as a children's author that she truly excelled. She had a natural talent thanks to an extraordinary imagination and an ability to make children laugh. No one was safe from her mischievous characterisations. Whether interviewing celebrities or catering for tennis players and BBC colleagues of Max during the Wimbledon fortnight, Liza never stopped observing and filing away characters for her next book. Her family was not exempt, they all became Wombles.

Despite her success, Liza, never really believed in herself. Her public face was one of charm; she was flirtatious, a joker and put people at ease, but in her diaries she confided doubts, depression, worry and fatigue. She was highly intelligent but berated herself for her idiocy. She did well in her School Cert and could have gone to Oxford, but there was no money and there was a war on and so she joined the WRNS as soon as she was old enough. With three brilliant older brothers – she was the youngest child by nine years – and not allowed to see her father once he had divorced her mother – her self-belief was not encouraged.

The first person to recognise her potential was 'Woody', her first boss in civvy street. Mr Woodham was a journalist in the Conservative Central Office Publicity Department, where Liza went as a shorthand typist on three guineas a week. He began to give her items to write up rather than type up, and interviews to do. Liza realised she had found her vocation.

Luckily for thousands of children around the world – her books were translated into many languages – her talent shone through and perceptive publishers gave her the opportunity and confidence to write books and then television serials and radio plays. Her output was phenomenal with 150 books to her name or as a contributor, hundreds – perhaps thousands – of articles and radio interviews, and *The Wombles*.

And on top of all that, she was a terrific, funny and loving mother to my brother Marcus and me. As a child I can remember my mother typing away in her study, which was no more than a dressing-room off my parents' bedroom, above the front door and overlooking the front garden and busy Earlsfield Road in south-west London. We children knew about deadlines and tried not to interrupt until she emerged from her world. In the holidays we would make up games in the nursery or garden and she would come and join in the fun when she had finished whatever it was she was working on.

It has been something of a revelatory process reading some of her letters and diaries. I have relived the highs and lows of my mother's life and I hope that I have achieved some objectivity. She began making extensive notes for her autobiography but she only got as far as her marriage to Max. I have included her memories wherever possible and tried to tell the story of her life in the manner of a memoir rather than a definitive biography. Some people who knew her may be dismayed that I have not written a hagiography, but rather' a 'warts and all' story of her life, yet I can assure them and all her fans that it is written with love and admiration for a remarkable mother and author.

Chapter 1

JD's Daughter

There were very few moments in Liza's life that were uneventful and her birth was no exception. Her parents, John Davys Beresford ('JD'), a successful author, and his wife Beatrice Evelyn (Trissie), were living a peripatetic existence in France and had taken up brief residence in Neuilly, Paris. Trissie was 46 when she gave birth to her fourth and final child, the only girl, on 6 August 1926. In the Beresford tradition she was named Elizabeth, and all was well – except neither parent thought to register her birth. Gendarmes were dispatched from the Hôtel de Ville to enquire why M. Beresford had not registered his daughter, 'Because I don't believe in bureaucracy,' replied JD. According to Liza, he was asked to accompany them to the gendarmerie and spent the night there, playing cards, while M. Le Maire was asked to produce some form of official validation of the baby's birth. The Mayor's letter remained thereafter the only legal evidence of Liza's birth and caused many a bureaucratic hiccup when she applied for a British Passport later on. The French spelling of her name, 'Elisabeth', remained with her for the rest of her life.

Liza's birth coincided with the beginning of the end of her parents' marriage, although not apparent to anyone at the time. JD and Trissie had met in London in 1910. He was the second son of the Revd John James, a Minor Canon of Peterborough and Rector of Castor, and his wife, Adelaide Elizabeth Morgan (of Morgan's Port). The Rev'd James, Liza's grandfather, was born in the reign of George IV in 1821, an extraordinary stretch of generations. At the age of 6, JD contracted polio (Infantile Paralysis) after swimming in a river, which left one leg underdeveloped and meant he had to use crutches for the rest of his life. Despite the crutches he was very athletic; as a young man he would cover twenty miles a day, and still nimbly swing himself and his crutches over a high gate when he was over 70.

In the spartan manner of a Victorian patriarch, Canon James believed that JD, younger son and an invalid, would have to shift for himself. His hopes were invested in JD's older brother, Richard Augustus Agincourt, who went to Oundle and on to Cambridge and later started a successful prep school, Lydgate House. JD, educated at a Dame School and briefly at Oundle, left school at 16 and was dispatched to be an architect's apprentice. In 1895 he completed his apprenticeship and having had more than his fill of the cold Norfolk rectory and his parents' frosty marriage, he joined a practice in London specialising in the design of hospitals. This gave him an income of about £2 a week, but his fond mother used to slide some cash his way whenever she could and he had some letters of introduction to the great and the good. One of them was Lady Sackville who lived in Ebury Street. JD accepted her invitations to lunch with alacrity, although there was one slight drawback, his hostess *always* ate al fresco in the back garden. It didn't put JD off for a moment. He ate his way steadily though the seasons, even on one occasion when it was snowing and he had to keep dusting the flakes off his plate. 'I remember, the butler coming towards us through a blizzard. He never lost his dignity and I never missed a mouthful', JD told Liza.

After eight years, during which JD honed his talent for draughtsmanship, he resigned, still seeking that elusive spirit of a path in life. By all accounts he was very charming, good-looking, and had a great sense of humour; he was also shy and lacking in self-belief. He tried selling life insurance, clerking in the tourist department of WH Smith, and producing copy for a publicity agent before starting to write fiction. He met and married an actress eight years older than himself, through whom he met actors and actor managers which led him to try his hand at playwriting and then, more successfully, novels.

These novels had early critical success, which did not necessarily provide an income but opened the doors of the literary salons of the day. In Naomi Royde-Smith's drawing-room he met W.B. Yeats, Aldous Huxley and Edith Sitwell among others. 'I was too much in awe of them to attempt to make conversation. But then, for many years afterwards, I was woefully lacking in self-confidence,' JD wrote in his *Memoir*. There were friendships from this time that became lifelong, HG Wells, Hugh Walpole, and especially Walter de la Mare, whom Liza described as an honorary godfather. JD's first wife was not an intellectual and preferred gaiety to literary longueur and eventually she asked JD for a divorce, much to his relief, but by then he had met Trissie Roskams at his North London lodgings.

Trissie was seven years younger than JD, born in 1880, and came from a very different background to her future husband. Her father, John Roskams, was 'in trade', a clothing manufacturer in Bristol. His twin passions seem to have been cricket and whisky. Liza wrote that, 'He often took my mother to watch his friend W.G. Grace in action.' She remembered Grace as fat and ferociously bad-tempered, and 'Grandfather lost an eye standing up to his fast bowling.' Trissie's mother died in her twenties from an illness apparently caught by eating contaminated watercress, leaving a widower and five children with Trissie, at the age of 10, responsible for her siblings. Two years later, her father married again, a pretty and very fashion-conscious girl.

She was not at all a wicked stepmother, but she and Trissie had little in common. Trissie, with all her energy, was bored by the endless visiting, the leaving of cards and the provincial social round. She threw herself into charity work, most of it to do with the local church where her father was a sidesman. Unfortunately he often had a few nips before the service and his family had an anxious time trying to stop him snoring too loudly.

But what could Trissie do with all that energy? Her education had been sketchy because no school would keep her for long. She went to sixteen altogether and although she said she was never actually expelled it must have been a close run thing, and she certainly ran away from several of them. When they had governesses at home she and her sister Lily made their lives such hell the wretched women only lasted for brief periods. So, at the age of 16, Trissie was allowed to put her hair up, do the flowers, go visiting, play the piano – rather badly – play tennis wearing long skirts, a corset and a bustle, and ride a bicycle. She loved cycling, the only drawback was she never learnt how to get off so she just pedalled straight at her nearest and dearest and expected them to catch her.

Trissie was not prepared to sacrifice herself to keeping house for her inebriate father and a stepmother not much older than herself. She wanted to get away from the endless chores at home so she decided to become a nurse in London. Her new career lasted three weeks. If the patients were very ill she couldn't bear it. If they were recovering she would wait until the sister was out of the ward and then seize hold of the luckless person and shake them, saying in a furious whisper, 'For goodness sake, get WELL.'

It was a technique she was to use on her own children years later. 'We never were ill,' Liza recalled. 'It wasn't worth the hassle. When I was about 9 or 10 I had all the classic symptoms of appendicitis: a grinding pain, being sick and feeling awful. Mother heard me out and then said: "We don't have appendicitis in this family, Elisabeth", so we didn't.'

Whether the hospital sacked her or she walked out is unknown, but she was steadfastly determined not to return to Bristol at any price. She fell in with a childhood friend, Eva Fellowes, who ran a boarding house for theatricals with her sister, and so Trissie moved in. Eva was also working as a waitress in a small restaurant in Baker Street which specialised in lunches for businessmen. Trissie became a waitress too and, although totally untaught, took her turn at cooking. She soon discovered she was a born cook and she loved it.

Mrs Marshall, probably one of the greatest cooks since Mrs Beaton, had set up a School of Cookery and, luckily for Trissie, she met one of Mrs Marshall's assistants who persuaded her to use her off-duty time to take lessons. Trissie collected recipes and ideas like a magpie and I still have her large, fat notebook which is full of handwritten recipes. Mrs Marshall's and/or Trissie's cheese straws were unbeatable, as were Liza's decades later.

It was in the boarding house that she met JD. 'The first thing I ever knew about him,' said Trissie, 'was the sound of him laughing as he went up the stairs.' There is nothing more seductive than laughter and it is perfectly possible to imagine the provincial Trissie, freed from the constraints of her family in Bristol, finding the witty but shy, clever but lame writer with flashing blue eyes, very attractive. He would have appealed to her motherly instincts as someone who needed looking after. She was vivacious and pretty and JD seems to have been an innocent abroad where romance was concerned and perhaps he recognised her practical qualities. There was no intellectual meeting of minds nor belief: JD had grown away from the beliefs of his parents while Trissie was a staunch Anglo-Catholic.

Then Trissie did a very daring thing. JD had taken a house in Cornwall and he begged her to leave London and join him. He was still awaiting his divorce so it was a very improper request – and one she acquiesced to at first, getting as far as St Pancras before her scruples or fears got the better of her and she returned to Swiss Cottage. Eventually, Trissie's propriety won the day; she and JD were married in April 1913 and they moved to Cornwall.

As JD's literary reputation grew, other authors became friends and joined the Beresfords there. Not all visits were successful and one indelibly printed on Trissie's mind was 'The case of the sloe gin and D.H. Lawrence.' JD was a socialist by instinct and the two men had a great deal in common, but Trissie and Lawrence were chalk and cheese. An early feminist, she was furious with him for not being kinder to his wife, Freida, who would sit silently at meals with the tears running down her face and into the soup.

Trissie had put down bottles and bottles of sloe gin to be opened on the 21st birthday of her eldest son Tristram. He was about 9 months old at this time so she was thinking ahead. In the winter of 1914 they let Lawrence have the cottage at a minimal, probably non-existent, rent as he was even more hard-up than they were. When Trissie returned from London the following spring, the lock on the sideboard had been broken and all the sloe gin drunk. She never forgave Lawrence. When he died he left her some Japanese vases and prints. It didn't make any difference to her opinion of him.

Hugh Walpole, too, stayed at the cottage. At that time he was being pursued by a most determined woman and Walpole, a gentle character and homosexual, was terrified of her. He followed Trissie from room to room saying, 'Don't leave me, Trissie, don't leave me alone with her. She's a tiger.'

'It was very difficult,' Trissie told Liza. 'Every time I left the kitchen for the sitting room there was Hugh, treading on my heels. I had to tell your Father in the end and he took him off for long walks across the sands but she followed them…' Eventually the tiger gave up on Walpole and married an ambassador instead.

Slowly, JD was starting to find his own voice in the literary world. His first novel, *The Early History of Jacob Stahl*, was published in 1911 and his second, *The Hampdenshire Wonder*, followed in the same year. He was also working as chief reader for Collins, the publishers, and for literary magazines, and although none of it was well paid he was starting to make a name for himself, and to make a much wider circle of friends such as Henry Williamson, Eleanor Farjeon (who years later became Liza's Godmother and a great friend to her when she was a child), Katherine

Mansfield, Aldous Huxley, Bertrand Russell and Walter de la Mare. The pressure of work was enormous and for five years he was dealing with approximately forty manuscripts a week for Collins, apart from his own writing. In 1916 the Beresfords' second son, Aden Noel, was born on Christmas Eve, followed two years later by Marcus James, who was to become a very successful writer himself, working in America under the name of Marc Brandel.

In 1923 JD was badly in need of a break. He'd had enough of reading piles of mainly mediocre manuscripts and he decided to resign from Collins and to take his family to live in France where he would write. Over the next four years they lived in St Maxime, Cannes, St Gervais, Arachon, St Jean de Luz, Paris and Dinard. While JD loved it in France, Trissie returned to England still without a word of French apart from bebé, which was Liza's pet name for years.

The Beresfords' quality of life on the Continent was comfortable. JD was writing well and successfully, the three boys were all boarders at their Uncle Dick's Prep School, Lydgate House, in Norfolk, but had a succession of servants and governesses during the holidays. The most memorable was Mademoiselle Gagnebin who had fled from the Bolsheviks with her Russian employers. She spoke eight languages, of which she said English was the most difficult. She went to Trissie in tears: 'I don't understand. You all of you say all the time 'he is a frenomine' – what does it *mean*?' It was eventually translated into 'friend of mine'.

In the holidays, Liza's brothers were renowned for getting into scrapes. One of her parents' most embarrassing moments was when brothers Aden and Marcus, conducting a purely scientific experiment, somehow managed to produce a short circuit which blacked out part of the Riviera. Their parents were at a dinner party and the moment the lights started to flicker they looked at each other and with sinking parental instinct. Up and down the Mediterranean coast the lights dimmed, grew brighter, and then died.

Aden and Marcus were an inseparable duo who were intelligent, looked angelic and could easily have turned their talents to criminality. Tristram, the eldest, was highly intelligent, grew to 6ft 3½ inches, had thick red-gold hair and was the apple of JD's eye. 'He was so handsome people used to stand in the street and just stare at him,' Liza used to say. He wrote a successful novel, *Break of Day*, when he was still at Cambridge, had a distinguished career including being an equerry to the Duke of Edinburgh at Buckingham Palace. He was awarded the CBE (for services to agriculture) and remained rather aloof from his siblings, who were possibly something of an embarrassment.

Aden, on the other hand, was the apple of his mother's eye, she adored him. From a very early age he was endlessly inventive and was rarely parted from the Meccano set with which he later made his little sister a series of toys, including an adaptable drawing machine. She loved the toys, but there was a catch; Aden would often run out of vital spare parts for his next invention and would have to pillage her toy cupboard, so nothing lasted more than a few days. With his large, innocent blue eyes and short blond hair he looked angelic and got away with mayhem. Later on it worked very well with girls when he and Marcus became a formidable duo. Marcus had red hair and freckles, the gift of the gab and, according to Liza, 'He didn't always seem to know right from wrong and later on got into real trouble with the law, at one point ending up in a Mexican gaol.' He also had several wives.

The Beresfords were a very interesting, somewhat eccentric family and it is easy with hindsight to see how great the financial opportunities were, but JD had no financial judgement at all. When he was approached about buying a very attractive villa on the Mediterranean for a most reasonable amount, he said, 'The South of France will never catch on.' He said exactly the same thing when he was offered shares in a new American business which was just starting up. It was known as the 'Threepenny and Sixpenny Stores'. 'It'll never catch on,' JD said, turning down Woolworths' original shares. A relation, an architect, offered him shares in a North London building development. He declined. It was Golders Green.

The family returned to England when Liza was nearly 3. They moved to rented accommodation in London for a couple of years and then to Ickleford Rectory, Hertfordshire, a rather rambling Victorian house with gardens, a dilapidated tennis court, a private path to the Rectory and a 'sad-eyed' gardener. When they arrived, all the staff were waiting by the front steps, including Annie Rhodes, who was to be Liza's nanny and to whom she remained devoted until her death in the 1970s.

It was here that Liza could first remember being the small, willing victim of Aden and Marcus. 'We're going to time your face flannel,'

Aden explained. 'We're putting it down the plug hole in the bath and you've got to run as fast as you can downstairs to catch it in the drain. One, two, three, go!' She just made it. This was the first of many such fraternal experiments which Liza recalled. When, many decades later, she invented the Womble characters, her brother Aden was the prototype of Tobermory, the Womble who can fix and invent all sorts of gadgets out of recycled rubbish.

With three sons at prep school and Tristram soon off to Oundle public school, JD was writing books and articles at a furious pace; the family were still living comfortably and unaware of the gathering storm clouds. For the children, the Rectory had plenty of advantages such as a tree house where Aden and Marcus took refuge when one of their scams went wrong.

Unfortunately, JD's fortunes began to wane as his books fell out of fashion and they had to leave the Rectory, moving in the early 1930s to Eaton Place in Kemp Town, Brighton (the Rectory was eventually pulled down and redeveloped into a housing estate). Their new home was conveniently close to Brighton College, renowned for its maths teaching, where Aden, a very good mathematician became a day-boy. As far as Liza was concerned Brighton was wonderful because for the first time she became aware of the sea, for which she developed a lifelong passion. She recalled:

I loved it, at night you could hear the growl of the waves as they pulled backward and forwards across the shingle, and there was always the taste of salt in the air, and it was scattered across the windows with the gulls wheeling and screeching overhead. And I became fanatical about bathing. When I finally mastered breast stroke I set out instantly for France. Fortunately somebody spotted me as I reached the end of the Banjo Groyne and a bad-tempered fisherman was sent off in pursuit. I didn't understand what all the fuss was about.

Liza became a day-girl at St Mary's Hall, Kemp Town. The school was started in 1836 for the 'daughters of clergymen', and Liza was admitted on a reduced fee as the granddaughter of a canon. She had very happy memories of St Mary's and decades later she was invited back to give a talk. The school was merged with Roedean in 2009 and the buildings sold to the Royal Sussex Hospital.

The Beresford's new home had the three top floors of a bow-fronted house on the corner of a street which led down to The Front. The house's height and position provided some unexpected bonuses for the boys. There was an outside goods lift at the back of the house; tradesmen went through a small back door, put their goods into the lift, latched it shut, shouted or whistled, and slowly turned a large handle until the lumbering lift reached a small hatch outside the kitchen windows, where the cook unlatched the hatch door and unloaded.

It was a laborious way of doing things, but it worked well – so well in fact that Aden hit on the idea that it could become a passenger lift. Liza recalled:

Annie must have been on her afternoon off when Aden, his blue eyes shining with the innocent light of the true inventor, said that I should be the very first passenger. It was, he said, really a *great* honour. They bundled me in, latched the door and began turning the wheel. It was quite an interesting feeling groaning upwards and watching the outside wall of the house crawl by. The only snag was that it stopped three feet short of the kitchen hatch when something diverted their attention and they abandoned the winch. They locked the wheel – luckily for me – and went off. I got pretty bored after a while and started shouting. A small interested crowd gathered in the street until somebody fetched the cook who was very cross as she'd been expecting vegetables and not a small, grubby girl. To her credit she never split on us, however she must have put the fear of God into the boys because there were no more lift experiments.

Aden, a true scientist, was not dismayed. His next brilliant idea was to test the strength of the bannisters. 'Now all we want you to do,' he said in his reasonable way, 'is to have an indoor *swing*. You'll like that.' They tied two skipping ropes together, knotted them to the banister, padded Liza up with cushions and lowered her over the deep, narrow well of the stairs where she hung suspended, a small, happy bundle. As the experiment lost its interest and the young scientists went off in search of other ideas, she swung on, got bored, and when the luckless cook happened to pass across the hall, three storeys down, she called out to her. The cook had hysterics, and Liza – rather unfairly – was sent to bed supperless. And so were the boys.

But that didn't stop them for long. At the rear of the top floor was an easily accessible roof with a small parapet running round it. For his own inscrutable reasons, Aden spent a lot of his time out there and he seemed to like his little sister's silent, unquestioning companionship. He was working on an experiment to do with the theory of gravity. Liza's job was to drop a selection of soft toys off the parapet at given intervals. She stood on the edge with the toys and began to drop them, leaning well over just to make sure they were on target. It must have been on about the fourth drop that Miss Wickens, who lived in the basement five floors down, came out of her back door. Although she wasn't exactly hit by a large white furry toy dog called Jim, he must have been travelling at a fair speed when he whistled past her and hit the ground. Understandably, Miss Wickens jumped violently, looked up and saw a small, fat figure waving to her on the sky line. 'Is she dead?' Aden asked with the detachment of the true scientist. Liza lent over further to make sure. It was Miss Wickens turn to have hysterics. The roof was put out of bounds and once again Liza was sent to bed.

Then there was the mystery of the runaway cart horses and a distant broken lavatory window. Aden and Marcus had been given air guns by some misguided relation. Diagonally across from the back of the house was a carriers' depot where all the goods were delivered by two enormous carthorses. The carter climbed down and started unloading. The sight of those two large rumps and their fly-twitching tails was irresistible to the two Beresford boys. The marksmen lay on on the forbidden roof, took careful air and fired. The unfortunate dray horses took off down the road at speed and were not stopped for a good quarter of a mile, scattering traffic and people and, miraculously, injuring no one. The uncharacteristic behaviour was eventually put down to flies and the heat of the day.

The sharpshooters might have got away with it if they hadn't been ambitious. They set their sights on a distant frosted-glass window. They took careful aim and shattered it. Another local mystery. The window happened to belong to a family acquaintance whom the boys didn't like much, and they made the great mistake of shattering it twice more. But by then the house owner had proved their match and he had taken sightings. The sharpshooters were caught literally bang to rights, the airguns were confiscated (forever), and for once Liza wasn't the one who was sent to bed.

It didn't put them off for long. They merely took up peashooters and a different firing range. Aden had grown tired of gravity experiments and had moved on to a new field.

'Now listen, Lizzy,' he said gravely. 'I just want to see how many volts a person can take and you're going to help me.' Liza didn't understand, but as usual believed in every word he said. 'All you have to do is to hold on to the two nice little handles and I'll give you a nice little shock. It won't hurt or anything but just say if it tickles too much. OK?'

Aden plugged in the wires and turned a dial. Liza recorded:

I don't remember too much about what happened after that, except that Marcus suddenly appeared, wanting to know what the fun was about. He took over my role, not without difficulty as I was apparently glued to the handles. Aden turned up the current… It may well have been Daddy swinging up the stairs on his crutches three at a time which stopped Marcus from being electrocuted. I certainly do remember his red hair standing on end by the time Daddy reached us.

That particular experiment was banned, but there were still plenty of other fields to be explored, one of which was the cinema.

The boys were mad about films and in the holidays when they got their pocket money they would vanish into The Odeon at 1.50 pm and leave at 10.30 pm having seen the programme round three times. They would return home red-eyed and practically word perfect. JD nearly had heart failure when Marcus said at breakfast, 'Did you know that Claudette Colbert's legs are insured for £10,000?'

'Is that what we send you to expensive public schools to learn?'

There was quite a heated discussion, but JD couldn't really keep it up because he too loved the cinema and anyway, Trissie felt it was about time that Liza too was taken to a see a film. Still remarkably innocent in the ways of her children, she asked Marcus's advice. He was a tremendous film buff (years later he made a very good living as a scriptwriter in Hollywood) said The Aquarium which, according to him, was showing *Puss in Boots*.

Liza was enormously excited when she and Trissie set off to catch the bus that trundled along the Front.

This was quite an adventure in itself as the camber was like a cross-section of the globe and the two-storey buses had a considerable tilt. If you sat just inside the bus with your back to the sea you were pinned in place by gravity, while the passengers opposite had to hang on for dear life as they leant forward. The top deck was open and it if rained you had to unroll a cover which was fastened to the back of the next seat and button it round your shoulders so that all that got wet was your head.

I loved it up on the top deck, but Mother wasn't keen on stairs as we had more than enough of them at home. A few years later during the war, I was coming home from school, sitting in the top front seat which fortunately had a roof over it by then, when it was spotted by a German fighter pilot. Obviously it made good target practice and he strafed it with machine-gun fire which made little impression on me as I had weightier problems on my mind like prep. Our headmistress, Miss Lockley, learned all about it and we were issued with a stern warning NEVER to sit on the top deck again. Of course this made it sound both exciting and immoral so naturally we continued travelling on the top deck, having stuffed our school hats into our blazer pockets, fondly believing nobody would be able to identify us.

Trissie and Liza arrived at the Aquarium shortly after the main feature film had started and stumbled to their seats in the flickering gloom. After a little difficulty with her seat – which would keep swinging shut so that all she could see were her feet pointing at the ceiling – Liza settled down.

There wasn't much evidence of Puss or his Boots on the screen instead there was a woman wearing a long nightdress and an agonised expression, which was hardly surprising as she was lying on a sofa in the middle of a jungle with a snake slithering round her ankles. Higher and higher went the snake and the girl rolled her eyes more and more, although she didn't seem able to do much else. Mother did though. She came out of a state of shock, snapped my seat shut so that my feet shot upwards again and hissed 'Close you eyes!' There wasn't much point really as all I could see were my feet and the ceiling. Mother, having paid her one and ten pence, plus ninepence, came to a rapid decision, we must stay put and wait for Daddy. He never appeared but I was eventually allowed to watch the *News* until there was a boxing item.

Under the seat, shut your eyes and cover your ears, Elisabeth!

Trissie's injunction had a lifelong effect on Liza and when, many years later, if she was watching BBC Sport on television and it switched to boxing, she automatically slid down to the floor, eyes shut, and ears averted. In 1956, under desperate circumstances, Liza was a very temporary boxing correspondent at the Melbourne Olympics. 'I was probably the first female reporter of the sport and certainly the only one who did the job not watching while the cameraman hissed what was happening in my ear.'

JD loved the cinema but hated going alone. Come hell, high-water or even a publisher's deadline, he went to the Savoy Cinema on Friday afternoons. It was quite a business and he usually took a very reluctant, shy and embarrassed Aden with him. JD would telephone the manager to say he was coming. Then with a hangdog son trailing after him, he would walk rapidly up the main road where he stepped briskly out from the pavement, holding out one of his crutches to stop the first bus that came along. He must have known about bus stops which ordinary people used, but he just didn't bother with them. Buses to him were merely large red taxis and amazingly enough, they always behaved like them and stopped. Aden would slink into the bus, where JD's crutches were neatly stowed under the stairs. Worse was still to come because as if hypnotised, the driver would stop as near to the cinemas as possible where the manager and an usherette were waiting in the foyer to show them to an aisle seat in the stalls. This special treatment, which was accorded to JD as a local celebrity, did not stop there.

'Tea at 4 o'clock,' JD would order briskly, and at four, to the minute, the usherette would come clanking down the aisle with a laden tray. Tea pot, hot water jug, milk jug, cups and saucers, sugar bowl, biscuits, the attention of the audience would be divided between JD, Aden, and what was happening on the flickering screen. JD's attention never wavered. His eyes were fixed firmly on Clark Gable or Jean Harlow, or possibly both, as he poured out the tea. Unfortunately his aim wasn't always true and more than once Aden got the hot water poured over his knees. A fate which he bore in unclenching silence until he got home. Eventually even his nerve snapped and Liza was happily seconded to Savoy duties.

Occasionally Hollywood stars came into Brighton's orbit. Tom Mix obligingly rode his horse up and down the steps of one of Brighton's grandest hotels, and Robert Taylor once brought Rottingdean to a complete standstill. Aden and Marcus had naturally been in the thick of it and gave a graphic description of it to Athene Syler, an elderly actress friend of Trissie's. Athene didn't think much of film people's acting, citing some of the supporting players in Eddie Cantor's *Roman Scandals*. Marcus, who had what must have been almost total recall of every film he'd ever seen, began to argue and an awkward situation was avoided by Aden saying gently, 'Oh but you saw the film in Birmingham. It was probably a different company.'

'Dear boy,' said Athene, 'Of *course*. Now why didn't I think of that!'

Somehow Marcus managed to get himself a holiday job as the tea-boy-come-assistant cameraman in the studios where Douglas Fairbanks was filming. What was more, Fairbanks actually wore Marcus's overcoat draped over his shoulders in one shot. The entire family trooped to the cinema to see the magic moment when the coat appeared.

Brighton in the Thirties was bursting with entertainment. There were a lot of cinemas, ranging from the local fleapit where you could get a seat for a few pence – or for two jam jars if you didn't mind sitting practically underneath the screen and getting a splitting headache and probably fleas. At the other end of the scale were the really grand picture palaces with organists playing a Mighty Wurlitzer that rose up mysteriously in front of the screen during the interval. The managers wore dinner jackets even for matinées, and the usherettes wore silver-buttoned uniforms and pillbox caps, and the restaurants had palm trees. There were also some very good theatres, of which the lovely Theatre Royal was 'the tops'. Quite often they presented plays just prior to their West End productions, so that the best acting in the world was available for half-a-crown, if you didn't mind climbing the almost perpendicular stairs and sitting in the gods, There was variety and music hall at the Hippodrome, and spectacular pantomimes at the end of the Palace Pier.

There was also the SS Marina Ice Rink, which became the next passion in Liza'a life because Sonya Hennie, the skating film star, was her idol. By polishing up the lino on her bedroom floor and wearing socks, Liza reckoned she could do quite a reasonable figure eight, although a 'spread eagle' with arms wide and one leg raised, usually ended in a painful nose dive onto the fender.

Liza, with her four best friends – twin sisters Angela and Rosemary and their cousins Alan and Gerald – could never quite raise enough money between them to pay for five season tickets to the rink, so they evolved a sure-fire method of getting in. Taking it in turns, the chosen four would march in with their tickets. If they were two boys and two girls, one of the girls would go to the Ladies, climb up and push her ticket out of the window. Down below in the street, the third girl would be waiting and would scoop it up and present it at the ticket office. It never failed and the five of them would reunite to go speeding round the rink, sometimes forming the forbidden 'chain'. The skater at one end of the chain would hardly move at all, but the last skater to join the line had to go very fast indeed as they were swung with increasing speed round the rink. Of course the day came when it happened to Liza. The forbidden chain was about twenty strong and she was travelling at the speed of an Olympic racer. Her shrieks and yells went unnoticed as she skidded over the ice, until the skater holding her hand caught on that something was wrong and let go. Liza zoomed over the ice, hit the barrier, went head over heels and ricocheted over the empty seats until finally coming to rest, upside down.

'Don't tell mother,' she sobbed as they reassembled her.

This conspiracy of silence worked pretty well. Trissie never knew about the time when one of her sons got stuck half way up the cliffs at Black Rock and had to be rescued by the Fire Brigade. And she didn't learn for years that teenage Marcus, already six foot, auburn-haired and very good looking, had actually gone to a forbidden night-spot called Sherry's where he'd seen the Duke of Windsor climb onto the stage to play the saxophone and sing, *The music goes round and round...*

Or when Marcus and Aden went to a rather fast club called Drusilla's, which was raided by the police. The boys climbed out of the Gents and got away in someone else's car. Marcus was asked to a very grand Friday to Monday party which, as there was rumoured to be a member of the royal family present, made Trissie, a devout monarchist, swell with pride. Marcus returned bloody but unbowed. 'They *made* me go to *church*!' He said, '*Twice* on Sunday!' He never went back.

It was about then that Liza's oldest brother Tristram decided to bring culture into her life. He was head boy at Repton, taking prize after prize until at one speech day he was asked to stay on the platform as there was no point in him going back to his seat.

Liza recalled that:

Tristram's shadow fell over us all. He seemed to know everybody and he decided I should meet a few important people. Scrubbed, neat and silent I was taken to a large house in Sussex where there was a lot of building going on. Tristram and a rather older man paced up and down and I was called over to join them.

'Elisabeth,' said Tristram. 'This is Glyndebourne which will one day be a very famous Opera House and this is Mr Christie who is responsible for it.'

'Hello, little girl,' said Mr Christie, 'and do you like opera?'

'Oh yes!' I said rapturously, 'I *love* Gilbert & Sullivan.'

Sadly, there were to be no further visits as the Beresfords faced further economic problems. The Inland Revenue, having tasted blood, were after JD and unfortunately his books were not selling too well. Emergency measures had to be taken and Trissie started taking in paying guests who were refugees from the growing menace of the Nazis.

Liza decided she would do her bit towards fundraising and was discovered selling 'flags', small pieces of crêpe paper with pins stuck through them, outside the back door. Her proceeds towards family financial help were slightly less than a shilling when business was brought to a very abrupt halt by JD's admonitory hand on the scruff of her neck. He balanced himself on his crutches and shook her until her teeth rattled. However, she did have one small money-making talent and that was drawing.

She was rather religious at the time and all the drawings, faithfully placed on Trissie's pillow every night, were usually of Jesus surrounded by angels. Liza recalled:

I was pretty hot on angels, but there wasn't much cash in them until by lucky chance I hit a vein of gold, well copper. Working away at my angels in a rough book I was spotted by the lordly captain of Upper Three.

'I don't suppose you could draw me?' she enquired. Quick as a flash I produced a glamorous portrait. 'Not bad' she said, and went to show her cronies and suddenly I was inundated with requests for (glamorous) portraits. I thought things over while chewing my rubber – I got through about two a week as well as pencil and handkerchiefs, and once reduced a pair of gloves to mittens while watching a film – and slowly an idea took shape.

'I'll draw your life but you've got to give me the paper and the charge is a halfpenny.'

It was money for old rope. A folded piece of exercise paper produced page one babyhood, page two at school, page three an astonishingly glamorous creature in evening dress and high heels. The back page was a dear old soul leaning on a stick. The bottom only fell out of the market when the clients ran out. But it was profitable while it lasted, augmenting a weekly income of 6d which had to cover comics, sweets, colouring books and the family's birthday and Christmas presents.

This was the adult world, but like all children Liza and her friends had another, totally different existence about which their parents remained blissfully ignorant. Although they had no right to be there, they infiltrated the very select gardens of Sussex Square and Lewes Crescent by devious means such as leaning on a rather timid child who lived in the select square so her parents had a key. When this wasn't available they just climbed over the tall spiked railings. The upper garden was formally laid out with lawns, flowerbeds and very tall trees.

The seats were usually occupied by very old ladies with small, shivering dogs. They took no notice of the children – in fact they might as well have been invisible. This is a memory that reappears in Liza's children's fiction, especially *The Wombles*, where they remain invisible to people who are too wrapped up in their inner thoughts to notice them.

Brighton in the Thirties was like a many-layered cake. The top consisted of the very rich eccentrics who still somehow managed to have one foot in the pre-1914 world. The Beresfords employed a girl called Winifred who helped with the washing up and 'looked like a startled hare'. One of her brothers was a footman in the service of a countess who, for a few weeks of the year, lived in one of the beautiful bow-fronted houses further along the Front. When Winifred's brother suddenly became ill, she was summoned by the countess to go and deal with him immediately.

Trissie didn't take to this dictatorial demand but she had to bow to a superior commander and Winifred deserted the kitchen sink. What actually happened next is uncertain, but news filtered through that the footman's bedroom was no more than a cupboard under the stairs and he had obviously been ill-treated. He and Winfred were dispatched back to deepest Sussex from whence they came and for a short while Trissie was so disgusted at the countess's callous treatment of the footman, that she toyed with becoming a socialist. However, when the Beresfords were bidden to lunch with Miss Birch, an exceedingly rich old lady who lived on the borders of Brighton and Hove in a large mansion surrounded by spacious grounds, Trissie's politics swung through about 180 degrees. Liza recalled:

We ate lunch off antique plates which were tepid to the touch and there was a solid phalanx of footmen, one of whom winked at me and I immediately fell deeply in love with him. Miss Birch gave me an umbrella with a duck's head handle and then took me into the library where she pressed a button and a section of the shelves swung outwards and there was a door to a hidden cloakroom. It was the only time I've ever seen a false bookcase with titles like *Cliff Tales by I. Fell-Over*, *Broken Windows by Eva Brick* and *Murder Stories by Hugh Dunnit*. Miss Birch and I thought they were excruciatingly funny and we became firm friends and equals. It was as if life had moved in a full circle and she at the very end of hers came within touching distance of a stolid little girl for whom life was just beginning.

There was another memorable invitation to lunch. Haile Selassie, deposed Emperor of Abyssinia, lived in Lewes Crescent and his daughters were, like Liza, at St Mary's Hall.

The girls asked me to lunch and that was the grandest of all as food was served on solid gold plate which was always cold to the touch and there was a white-suited servant behind each chair. Once, walking home from school, the Emperor was just ahead of me. He was very small and somehow there was an air of overwhelming sadness about him. I've never forgotten it.

These brushes with the Brighton rich and high-born were infrequent interludes in Liza's childhood. Her sense of adventure, however, was a constant worry for her family Having climbed every tree in the gardens of Sussex Square and Lewes Crescent, and having ripped all her clothes in the process, which taught Liza how to mend, she set her sights on an even better climb: the roof of the house. They had moved to a four-storey house where they could take more lodgers. It was to prove a fatal mistake but Liza, at least, was happily unaware of the growing threat of war. She persuaded one of her friends to act as look-out at the bottom of the attic ladder.

I trod carefully across the dusty beams, pushed open the skylight and hauled myself up on to the narrow parapet. There were no Miss Timmins here to bombard with teddy bears, so after watching a few heads with legs go bobbing past, I decided to clamber up the steep slates which was quite difficult as they were slippery. However, I eventually reached the chimney stacks and sat down. The view was wonderful. There were all the other angular roofs of Kemp Town and in the distance the rolling Downs and Roedean, while over to the west, stretching into the sparkling sea, were the Palace Pier and the West Pier and beyond them the hazy blur of Shoreham.

Four storeys down Mother was happily playing bridge with her Ladies Four, all of them wearing afternoon dress and hats, when the phone rang and a trembling voice said, 'Mrs Beresford, you don't know me but I live opposite and I think I should tell you that your daughter is sitting on the roof.'

None of the boys were home so Daddy climbed the stairs on his crutches in record time, but was beaten by the step-ladder. Slowly a distant roaring sound reached me and reluctantly letting go of the chimney pots, I slithered down the slates, hit the foot-high parapet, teetered for a moment and then reached the skylight. I wondered why all the people in the street were gazing upwards and shortly discovered the answer. Daddy seized me by the scruff of the neck and with his crutches spread wide shook me yet again. Mother went on crying and my now ex-friend, the 'look out' was sent home under escort and I was sent to bed. As usual without the faintest idea what all the fuss was about, and read *Rupert* books under the bed clothes by torchlight.'

It was not a particularly happy household by the late Thirties, and the boys began to break away from it. JD had become a pacifist, a position reflected in his later books – and they were not popular. He was still doing a lot of book reviewing and one room in the house was put aside for the parcels of books which were sent to him. Liza was forbidden to go near them so naturally somehow managed to sneak in and read a great many of them. Some were highly unsuitable for a child, but she just bypassed what she didn't understand. She had become a passionate reader of anything and was besotted by Becky Sharp in *Vanity Fair* and always hoped that next time she read it there would be a happy ending for her.

While still at Cambridge, Tristram became engaged to a fellow undergraduate, Anne Stuart-Wortley. According to Liza she was lovely and got on well with all the family. She gave Liza a delicate little bracelet of turquoise and chip diamond, which she in turn passed on to me. It was part of a set given by Edward VII to Daisy, Countess of Warwick, who was a relation of Anne's. It was a wildly unsuitable 'bribe' for a 10-year-old tomboy, but Liza always loved it – and Anne too.

She was very good to me and asked me to stay in their house in Warwickshire when I became an aunt at the age of 11, and Tristram was an announcer at the BBC. Occasionally he was summoned to Broadcasting House and mother and I used to listen to every word. He acquired land and started cultivating it and ultimately ended up at Manor Farm near Salisbury with 1,000 acres. He became at one point the Chairman of the West of England NFU. But that was all way in the future.

Marcus, the real rebel of the family, became involved with the then rather erratic daughter of the even more unusual Lord Redesdale, and absconded to France with her. Liza used to say that, 'The runaways who were both 19 were brought back by her father and he and JD hated each other on sight. Sitting on the stairs, my head through the bannisters, I witnessed their furious argument in the hall while they both blamed each other's child.'

The daughter was a bit of a bolter as shortly afterward she went off again with another teenager, this time with a great fanfare of publicity. Years later, Marcus told Liza that he and the girl had remained the best of friends for the rest of their lives. It was the start of a series of romantic adventures and, as far as Aden and Liza were able to work out, he had five wives and various children living in Hollywood, Ireland, London and Mexico. He wrote books, plays and film scripts very successfully, but there were a few bad patches to begin with. He bolted from Cambridge after a year and somehow managed to get to America. Meanwhile Aden and Liza remained close, with Aden became something of a substitute father for her when JD finally left home in August 1939.

The difference in intellect on the one hand, and lack of income on the other, had been showing cracks in the Beresford marriage for many years. The rows got steadily worse until a full-blown fissure opened up between them. In Trissie's view, JD had selfishly pursued his spiritual quest in a way that was not only far removed from her own High Anglican orthodoxy, but also resulted in writing that was of no commercial value. He was a peaceful, considered man, but perhaps not proactive, and certainly not willing to take up the cudgels with his fiery wife. Trissie was frustrated by what she saw as his inactivity and inability to provide for his family in the way she expected. She was now a breadwinner at the beck and call of lodgers, while JD pursued his own intellectual interests. This pattern would later repeat itself, although not in quite the same way, in Liza's own marriage.

Living opposite the Beresfords was Esmé Wynne-Tyson, separated from her husband, and her teenage son Jon. Esmé, a childhood friend of Noel Coward, was a published writer and had less erudition than JD but a similar interest in enquiring after metaphysical truths. She and JD formed a deep friendship and eventually they became collaborators on nine books but Trissie, not surprisingly, referred to her as 'that woman', and despised her. Eventually, without premeditation, JD walked across the road taking nothing with him and lived with Esmé until his death in 1947.

Jon Wynn-Tyson and Liza had been the best of friends.

We had a 'telegraph' system on the top floor from his bedroom across the street to mine. We did it by the simple means of each lowering a ball of string meeting in the street and tying the string together and then up to our respective rooms and pulled it taut and tied off to a weight on the window sill together with a small hand bell. Whoever woke up first in the morning rang their bell to wake up the one opposite to make plans for the day, talking across the quiet of the fifth floor. People often stopped to gaze up at us and nobody ever worked out how we had done it.

Jon was kind to Liza and saved up his pocket money to take her out for a meal. They strolled along the Undercliff Walk where there was a boisterous wind and galloping waves. They started to run backwards to try to avoid a potential soaking, when Liza fell and was knocked out cold, causing concussion. As a result, part of her memory was wiped and she had only the vaguest recall of the terrible arguments between her parents in the evenings, during which she pulled all the bed clothes over her head trying to drown out the voices. Once JD had left, Trissie would make Liza stand by the window through which they could see his flat opposite at 6 Chichester Terrace, while she condemned JD and Esmé with harsh words that no 13-year-old should hear. Trissie saw herself as betrayed and could not believe that JD's cohabitation with Esmé was one of intellectual friendship and not an adulterous affair. It is easy to see with hindsight that there was misunderstanding and blame on both sides; but there was only one real casualty – Liza – as Tristram was by then married with a daughter, Marcus had made his way to the USA, and Aden was at Brighton Polytechnic. Trissie forbade Liza to see her father ever again and she never did.

Meanwhile the shadow of war began to move closer, although Liza remained happily unaware of the implications. She continued to skate and swim with her gang at the Blackrock pool where they managed to avoid the lifeguards' eagle eyes to jump off the top diving board and land flat on the water. 'It was extremely painful but I always hoped that by some miracle it would turn into a dive. It never did.'

Paranoia about Hitler and Germany was understandably rife in the UK in 1939, and Liza's gang became very spy-conscious so they decided to take action and do 'their bit' and tried to break in to a house that faced out to sea. The owners were often away and Liza and her friends wanted to find evidence of the owners' treachery. The gang was convinced that the 'spies' were signalling across the channel with the aid of an enormous glass plate mirror which they thought they could glimpse through the keyhole. Fortunately their break-in failed but they passed their fears onto the police who apparently kept a straight face but were not too concerned by the girls' report.

More and more rolls of barbed wire appeared and suddenly their beloved swimming pool was closed as was the Front and Lewis Crescent Gardens. Small gun posts were put up and Trissie had to have black-out curtains fitted. A number of Trissie's elderly residents decided they knew better than the Government and packed up and left for the West Country and the Lake District. This geriatric migration didn't filter through bureaucratic channels for a long while, which was good news for the rest of those living in the house as when rationing started they had far more food per capita than the normal allowance.

The entr'acte between peaceful preparations and the outbreak of war couldn't last, and the beginning of the end of their way of life and world came to a halt at the end of that long, warm summer in 1939. At the beginning of September, Brighton was designated a 'Safe Area' for evacuees from London and Trissie agreed to take in six evacuees, housed in what had once been JD's workshop. It was now that Liza ran into bureaucratic difficulties for not having a birth certificate or passport; the final identity card which was issued was of a different colour to others, giving Liza kudos at St Mary's Hall.

The first siren sounded on the morning of Sunday, 3 September, when Trissie and Liza were in church. War had not yet been declared (Prime Minister Neville Chamberlain broke the news in his radio speech at 11.15) and all the congregation rushed out of church and gazed up at the pale blue sky. There wasn't an aircraft in sight.

Liza thought it was exciting, but Trissie cried all the way home on the bus. Like so many of her generation, her family had lost young sons in the previous war, and now she had her immediate family to worry about. From then on she kept a sharp carving knife on the front kitchen table.

'Don't worry,' she used to tell Liza. 'I'll kill you before the Germans get to you.'

Meanwhile, Liza had mixed fortunes at St Mary's Hall. Miss Grey, the grandmotherly headmistress who had kept an eye on her, had retired and a Miss Stopford had taken her place. She and Trissie had become friends.

One day Liza got caught climbing out of a classroom window for a dare. It was such a dreadful crime that she was sent for by the assistant headmistress, who told her that as she also ate her school meals with her elbow sticking out there was no chance of her ever achieving much in life beyond becoming a form prefect in Upper Three. Shortly after that,

Liza nearly put an end to any chance of any career whatsoever. St Mary's Hall was over 100 years old and had beautifully polished – and lethal – stairs and corridors. One of the girls' best (and forbidden) games was to get up speed on a long passage and then to slide the rest of the way to the classroom at the far end. Unfortunately, when it came to Liza's turn someone closed the end door just as she took off. She zoomed down the corridor, realised far too late what had happened, and put out her hands to stop. As the top of the door was made of glass, the result was spectacular. The glass splintered across her wrist and to her amazement blood shot upwards like a fountain. While all of the girls were goggling at the phenomenon of being able to bleed like an oil gusher, a more intelligent senior, although rather green in the face, had the wits to clutch hold of Liza's arms and drag her to the matron, leaving a trail of blood all the way. Fortunately, it wasn't as serious as it could have been and she left with two heavily bandaged wrists.

It wasn't too long before Liza ran into more trouble. She and her four best friends had saved up and bought a much-loved, elderly bicycle for £1. When they got the balance right – which wasn't often – all five of them rode it together. One on the handlebars, one peddaling on the seat and two on the guard at the back. It took very careful timing to get them working in unison, but occasionally they did manage about five yards of erratic progress. The trouble was that nobody seemed to be in charge of the brakes, which became an important issue after they had hit several park benches, pedestrians, and very nearly decapitated a small dog.

This timeless period ended suddenly, with the evacuation of the British Army at Dunkirk. Liza wrote:

We were shaken out of our apathy not so much by the enormity of the situation but by a series of small local events. The fishmonger, a dour young man, suddenly vanished from his barrow.

'Gorn,' said his mother, a mountainous woman who wore a sacking apron and had a moustache. 'Over there...'

He had rowed his small fishing boat across the Channel, picked up survivors from the beaches and somehow brought them back. Our youngest lodger, a very diffident 19-year-old called Horace, vanished into the RAF to become a fighter pilot.

The wardens became a great deal stricter about the blackout, and everybody had to carry their gas mask. Nobody was allowed out after 9 pm except for a special reason. A number of strange, painted signs appeared: ARP, FAP, EWS. Large concrete structures were built along the Front and the grass courts at the tennis club (always referred to as a 'game of bats') were sub-contracted to goats.

> We covered our windows with more criss-cross sticky tape and one night the warden cycled round with his loud hailer telling us to leave our windows open. Later we found out why. There were some tremendous explosions which rattled everything. The middle of the Palace Pier and the West Pier had been blown up in case the Germans tried to land there.

Sandbags appeared around Brighton Town Hall; empty houses and some of the hotels were taken over by sailors and soldiers and very occasionally a small German aircraft would drop its bombs *before* the siren had started its melancholy wail. In gym lessons, the girls of St Mary's Hall were taught how to roll themselves into a small ball with their hands clasped behind their necks if they got caught in the streets in a sudden raid. There was another timeless period of waiting, and then the bombing began in earnest and life as Liza knew it was to change forever.

Chapter 2

War and Peace

It was a beautiful hot summer in 1940, with a blue sky which was often criss-crossed with the white trails it left behind by the remote dog-fights going on overhead. But is was still all very unreal to Liza until one September Saturday. St Mary Hall's headmistress, Miss Stopford, of whom Liza was terrified, had come to lunch with Trissie. Liza's brother Aden was home on leave and all four were in the first-floor sitting-room when the air-raid alarm sounded. Trissie drew the thick orange velvet curtains and put on the light. The lodgers were all in their rooms.

There was the distant crump-crump-crump of the anti-aircraft guns on the Front and then, quite suddenly and with no noise at all, Liza was lifted right across the room to land on top of a book case. The tattered remains of the curtains and a great deal of dust, plaster and glass floated down on the remains of the room. She never heard the bomb at all.

They had been hit by one of a stick of very small bombs. Like a dignified old lady shaking out her skirts, the house started to collapse on itself. Miraculously the only casualty was the cook, Edith, who had been resting her legs in her basement room when the ceiling descended on her. While she was being dug out, Trissie discovered that all the jam she had bottled that morning was now spread and splattered over the remains of the dining room. Shock, fright and fury combined to produce some totally uncharacteristic bad language and behaviour. Aden bundled Liza out into the street with stern instructions to look after cook's small nephew and niece, who clung to her like white mice. They were all covered in dust and plaster as they picked their trembling way over the glass-littered street which had been hit by five bombs. Liza recalled:

It resembled a demolition site. I saw my first dead body. It was our postman who had been killed by the blast. A small, neat man, even in death, he looked as though he was fast asleep, his eyes peacefully closed behind his unbroken spectacles. The letters were still in his hand.

'Was that your house, little girl? We'll get that bastard Hitler, don't you worry,' said the Warden and he actually shook his fist at the empty sky. 'You know, you never meet an atheist in an air raid.'

It was all unreal as the two children and 14-year-old Liza crouched together on a staircase.

I held onto them but they were too frightened to move. The rescuers worked desperately and got the cook out from under the rubble, shocked but miraculously unhurt. It was a kind of organised chaos as the men dug desperately with their ringing shovels while the glass shattered underfoot. People came and went and my beloved black and white cat, Whisky, was rescued but he was demented with shock as he ran in circles. One of the men killed him with his shovel. Aden went back into the house to see what he could rescue but there wasn't much and it was very unsafe. All my beloved toys vanished and I can still see and name all of them in my head. It's a scene which has never left me and is forever being repeated in my memory.

Trissie and Liza were taken in by elderly friends and Liza slept on the carpet under their piano. St Mary's Hall had already had some bomb damage and the girls were divided up between Roedean, Queen Anne's Caversham and St Catherine's Bramley. Liza was dispatched very quickly to St Catherine's, with what uniform that had been recovered from the Beresford's bombed house.

I really didn't know what was happening and just silently did as I was told. It was all unreal, especially as term hadn't yet started so there were no other girls, just a few staff. They were kind enough but very strict and I was forbidden to mention the bombing, God knows why. So when I was in the empty dormitory at night and heard a plane, or the ack-ack guns going off in the school grounds, I slept under my iron bedstead. I was desperately homesick but there was no home to write to. When the other boarders finally arrived for the Autumn Term, I really looked forward to it convinced that it would be like something out of the *Girl's Crystal*. But nobody bounced up to me saying 'Welcome to the Lower Fourth', in fact nobody spoke to me at all for a long time which gave me the eerie feeling that I was invisible.

The school was far more sophisticated than St Mary's Hall.

Some of the girls actually went to cocktail parties where they drank sherry and gin. For a long time I thought you drank them mixed. They also climbed out of the dormitory after dark and went to meet the ack-ack soldiers who were posted in the grounds. As I was the only girl in the school who wore nightdresses, I spent the entire term going to bed wearing the despised nightdress underneath my siren suit so no one could see I was not wearing pyjamas.

The headmistress, Agatha Symes, was a large, imposing woman with a slight limp and a walking stick.

'Here comes dot-and-carry-one' somebody would sing out as the familiar thump-clump echoed down the corridors, so that by the time she majestically appeared we all seemed to be working hard. As I was the newest pupil I was the last to get the use of a bathroom and you *had* to have a bath before evening chapel. Aden's training yet again proved invaluable. I could get in and out of tepid water in one minute flat and who cared about washing? Soap was rationed anyway. What with that and the siren suit I must have smelt like a ferret by the end of term. Drying time was non-existent and I would skid to my place in the chapel choir stalls before Miss Symes made her stately entry. Forever afterwards, singing 'thirds' in *Gloria in Excelsis* was bound up in my mind with slowly drying out. By the time we reached the last *Amen* I was literally home and dry.

One evening, wearing her beloved siren suit with the hood up, Liza went to say her prayers and knelt in the prayer stalls. The lighting was very dim and it was quiet and peaceful. Suddenly there was a scream and the thud of running footsteps which grew fainter and fainter. Liza followed.

I was halfway down the shadowy corridor when I heard the familiar thumping approaching and flattened myself into an alcove.

'I saw him, I saw him!' said a hysterical voice.

'Saw who?' demanded Dot-and-carry.

'The monk! The monk that haunts the chapel. He was there, kneeling in the prayer stalls!'

'Nonsense girl!' Dot-and-Carry and a senior prefect swept past me. I tip-toed off to the dormitory.

It was an enormous relief to Liza, and probably to the school too, when she left at the end of the term for the simple reason that Trissie, with no house and no lodgers, had no income and had run out of money. Mother and daughter became evacuees together.

If any evacuee in 1941 had had the choice of choosing the perfect person on whom to be billeted, they would have had to choose Miss Dampier, known as Damps. The story of their evacuation to Ditchling was retold by Liza in her children's book, *Lizzie's War* (Simon & Schuster 1993). She bore a great affection for the eccentric Miss Dampier throughout her life; it was a very happy interlude in Liza's turbulent childhood.

She was large, wore the most terrible clothes which were often held together by haphazard mending and safety pins and she had the kindly, puckered face of an elderly child. Anything that had happened in the world since 1918 was a kind of dream to her.

She was the daughter of an Admiral and had been brought up as the Edwardian, if not Victorian, daughter of a comfortable, protected family. She had been educated by governesses and knew very little about the outside world. She was already in her late middle age when her father died and she had to move into the real world. She had finally ended up in one half of a 1930s house in rural Sussex, but once having found herself there she loved it all enormously. She was totally impractical, knew nothing at all about housekeeping or cooking and would listen to Trissie with a look of placid bewilderment as she tried to explain the minefields of rationing. Coupons were a complete mystery to her. Having been told firmly by Trissie that they didn't have enough coupons for a chicken to feed her naval nephew on leave, Damps didn't turn a hair and the following day produced a large fowl from the bottom of her large, leather shopping bag. The fact that it was still warm, had all its feathers, and presumably its innards, didn't faze Damps in the least.

'I shall cook it. Leave it *all* to me,' she told a sceptical Trissie. Liza and her mother went for a walk and on their return saw dusky blue smoke coming out of the windows which smelled awful. Damps was standing in the kitchen, flapping her hands and saying plaintively: 'I don't understand it.'

'I do,' said Trissie, yanking open the oven door. There were the remains of a charred and feathered carcass on a priceless famille rose plate.

Somehow Trissie managed to extract the grisly remains and to make a meal out of them and Damps was enchanted by this expertise and thereafter wisely left Trissie to deal with the coupons and cooking, which improved enormously. Quite a lot of the food arrived after dark on the back of a bicycle, but the Beresfords asked no questions.

Damps had her own, very simple, formula for making marmalade stretch, she just poured the remains of the teapot into the jar. 'It certainly made the marmalade last longer and gave it an unusual flavour and a rather runny consistency. We both ate it just the same. But then I was always hungry and would eat anything,' Liza used to say.

Damps was also an enthusiastic gardener. Never having been allowed to do it before, she was a natural. She planted, dug and pruned. She didn't own an apron and her disreputable old clothes became even worse and she would sometimes mislay her jewellery. 'Many was the time I scrabbled around the potatoes or the fruit bushes and with luck everything would be recovered. I'll never forget the enchanted moment when in the evening light I saw a blackcurrant bush decorated with glittering rings.'

Liza adored her and so did her brother Aden when he visited for occasional weekend leave. Much to his delight he discovered that Damps had a car locked in her garage. In great anticipation, Aden unlocked the garage and then came reeling out again. Unfortunately Damps also stored her cider apples in a net suspended above the open-backed car; the apples had fermented, dropped into the car and rats, attracted by the smell, had eaten their fill.

'I'm afraid, Damps, that the car is full of very dead, alcoholic rats,' Aden reported.

'Dear me, well I daresay it was a very happy death...'

'I'm afraid the car's a wreck.'

'I never cared for it, dear boy. It was always hitting things.'

Damps taught Liza to take every day as it comes and never to worry if you misplace diamonds in a potato patch, or to fret if your car is loaded with dead rats, and that priceless famille rose doesn't have to be in cabinets. Liza never saw Damps anxious or upset about anything, and although her casual attitude to life occasionally drove practical Trissie mad, she improved their lives considerably at a very difficult time.

Liza's education was resumed with the Misses Dee who were sisters, both in their 80s, who ran what must have been one of the last Dame schools in England. They lived and behaved as if Edward the VII were still alive and living at Sandringham.

Mathematics was not considered a suitable subject for young ladies and to Aden this came as shocking news so he took Liza under his wing and set her page after page of calculations and formulae which she enjoyed, with the result that she was into calculus in her very early teens. *Mathematics for the Millions* was her favourite book for years afterwards and she always claimed that Aden, who was by then working for Sir Robert Watson Watt, wrote the outlines of radar theory on her bedroom wallpaper. The elder Miss Dee, who despised anybody who could even recite the ten times table was not impressed by Aden. 'Your sister would be better employed learning the names of Howards and the kings and queens of England!' was her (ladylike) robust advice. The seven senior pupils, aged 13 and 14, were sent off to explore the Sussex Downs to search for flowers, to pick one only and to press between sheets of blotting paper before putting it into their nature books. They discovered Ladies Slipper and the Queen Bee Orchids and rank outsiders Cowfold Umbiliferee, Toad Wort, Ox-Eye daises and every kind of clover.

Liza loved the Downs and would lie on the soft, spring turf watching the cloud shadows race across the flat countryside below. In the spring the skylarks hovered overhead while the grass riffled backwards and forwards. It was timeless and peaceful and solitary; during the winter, freak frosts on top of the Downs encased each blade of grass with ice, and as a small wind raced over them so each blade tapped against its neighbour, creating sharp, tinkling music, running sharp and flat and back again in wave after wave of sound. Liza thought it was as if the Downs were singing to each other.

Then one weekend, Aden and Liza climbed up onto the Downs and hadn't walked more than a couple of miles when suddenly they were surrounded by soldiers, wearing gas masks and carrying rifles. In eerie silence they were marched to the nearest windmill. A young officer, sitting behind a table and also wearing a gas mask, interviewed them in a muffled voice. Who were they? Where were they going? What were they doing there? It was all very strange and Liza hadn't the least idea what was going on or why. It seemed to her that she had been promoted to being a 13-year-old spy and the atmosphere was pretty tense until the interrogator said suddenly:

'I say, aren't you Aden Beresford? Outside please.'

Liza's vivid imagination ran away with her and she thought he was going to be shot. It seemed a very long time before Aden and the officer returned on very good terms. Aden and Liza were put in a van and driven home.

'Well, Lizzy,' Aden explained, 'It seems the Army were just behind us this morning. They were laying mines and we could have been blown up. I was at school with the captain.'

Sometimes on moonless nights, the Damps household could see the angry red light that glared over London and catch a fleeting glimpse of the criss-crossing searchlights. Liza's eldest brother Tristram, as well as farming flat out, was doing his part-time duty as a radio announcer at the BBC in London and when, in an emergency, he found himself working in Portland Place, was transfixed by the sight of rolls and rolls of barbed wire laid across the majestic, marbled entrance hall of Broadcasting House, with a one-armed soldier supposedly marching up and down.

'He could hardly keep on his feet,' said Tristram. 'He was sliding all over the place. He couldn't have stopped anyone!'

Trissie and Damps ignored this as 'subversive talk', and, like many other people, continued to believe that the war was just a momentary upset which would go away if one ignored it. Unfortunately, it became increasingly hard to ignore as supplies of food were growing shorter. Liza started to have adolescent yearnings not for Victor Mature or Tyrone Power, but cheese and sausages. At the Dame school, she and her classmates had problems concentrating on the kings and queens of England.

'Egbert eight thirty-seven,' they chorused, their minds not on the date of the Saxon kings, but on jam.

'All things bright and beautiful,' sang the younger Miss D in her deep bass voice as she pounded away on the ancient harmonium with many keys missing.

'All creatures great and small,' they sang, imagining pork pies, chips and ice-cream.

More and more army lorries and cars roared through Ditchling and then turned off up a long drive to a mysterious house. As all the vehicles had signs on the back which read *Max Speed 30 MPH*, Liza came to the conclusion that all the vehicles were owned by a man called Max Speed, aged 30. She and her friends thought it quite logical that as he had a considerable fleet he must be extremely rich and powerful and probably had mountains of black market food, so they started hanging about at the end of his drive in the hope that he would take pity on them.

To pass the time they practised 'flying eagles' on their bicycles, standing on the saddle with one foot while hanging on to the handlebars. Inevitably the day came when a van was forced to take a detour through a hedge to avoid them.

'Bloody kids. Git aaht of it!' shouted a furious voice from the bushes. As they pedalled forlornly back to the village, they became aware that a dog-fight of more than usual ferocity was taking place overhead. It didn't occur to them to take cover as the planes, guns rattling, dived and climbed until, with a final spin, began to corkscrew downwards. A parachute blossomed against the blue sky and an ancient farm worker armed with a pitchfork went in pursuit of it. The Spitfire did a victory roll and roared off while the pilotless plane produced an unearthly scream as it gathered speed.

The children abandoned their bikes and threw themselves into the nearest ditch. There was a tremendous explosion, a sheet of flame and a great deal of black smoke. Liza wrote that:

Ammunition zinged and rattled through the bushes sending leaves and bark flying like hail. When things had quietened down a little, we crept out to have a closer look. It was a chance not to be missed. We scavenged for trophies, most of which were still sizzling with heat. Occasionally something 'zinged' over our head. I had just acquired a really sensational piece of hot metal about two feet long and embedded with what looked like metal pea pods when above all the zinging and the crackling flames, there came the sound of pounding boots and furious voices. Treasure time was definitely over and we took to our heels.

Liza gave Damps her find who was really pleased and used it as a doorstop until the naval nephew came home on leave again and pointed out that it was part of a machine-gun containing live bullets.

Among the friends that Liza made in inland Sussex was a colony of artists who used to let her wander in and out of their studios and watch them at work. Sir Frank Brangwyn was one of them and he taught her a great deal. Thanks to him, she had one painting, *The Family*, of two adults and two children standing in a group and looking directly at the world, exhibited in a London gallery.

However, Liza's world was about to change yet again and her country idyll was coming to an end because in her sixties Trissie had found a job that came with a house in Brighton and they were evacuees no longer.

It was to take over as manager of a 'Ladies Club'. It was in Chichester Place, Brighton, in the next street to the one they had left so abruptly, and it was a job which fitted Trissie perfectly. It enabled her to use all her organising abilities to the full. She was a born manager and within a couple of months she had got the Ladies Club out of the red, acquired a devoted, elderly staff, including Alice the waitress who was 85, deaf, went to her 'social' every night, and could, at times, be mutinous. Trissie ruthlessly ousted the unsatisfactory paying guests and somehow improved the food to such an extent that the lodgers' friends were always angling for invitations and had to be put on a rota.

It wasn't too long before Trissie took over completely, severing her links with the Clubs Association and taking in a *male* lodger. Mr Thirkell was a shy, kindly soul, late of the Inland Revenue – which would have shaken JD but which held no qualms for Trissie. She was a corseted Victorian woman and she only had to sigh and look despondent for Mr Thirkell to ask if he could help, a trait which Liza inherited and used constantly in later life and one that would shock the sisterhood of the twenty-first century.

'I just don't understand arithmetic,' Trissie would say, which was quite true; it is doubtful if she ever did a sum in her life.

'Perhaps I could be of assistance?' suggested Mr Thirkell, happily replete after a miraculous three-course dinner, and that was another problem solved.

It was a pleasant house, double-fronted with a semi-basement where Liza lived and could lie in bed and watch feet go by. There were ten letting bedrooms, one bathroom, a minute garden at the back, a machine gun on the roof opposite and an enormous naval gun 50 yards down the road. It gave them a feeling of security but it was also rather inconvenient as any time it was fired it shattered their windows.

By 1941 Brighton had been designated a 'Danger Area'. It didn't seem to upset the town much, which remained beautiful and calm if getting shabbier and slightly war-damaged round her elegant facade. The remaining elderly inhabitants continued to walk slowly up and down what was left of the Front, their gas masks banging on their hips while they looked sideways at the increasing number of troops who were pouring into the town. The old retreated as the young moved in. The Metropole, the Grand, and the Norfolk hotels were all commandeered and there were unfamiliar uniforms and accents everywhere.

Rumours abounded about the licentiousness of the Poles/Czechs/ Dutch/French who seethed through the streets, and although Brighton residents were told endlessly to be friendly and polite to the glorious allies, Trissie felt that they were all too friendly given half a chance and she started keeping the ever-sharp carving knife on the kitchen table twenty-four hours a day.

Trissie settled down pretty comfortably to wartime conditions and a whole new part of her character blossomed as she found her size three feet in not so much the black market, but more a shade-of-grey market. For instance, although she wouldn't have considered – at this point anyway – buying coupons, there was a subtle way round the problem, namely the 'Pig Man'.

He called very early every Saturday morning in his battered van to cart off all the edible remains such as old cabbage leaves, stalks, potato peelings and so on, back to his Sussex pig farm. Trissie would somehow manage to cook him a delicious breakfast and the pig man would gaze at her admiringly as she fussed over him, listened to his troubles and gently hinted at some of her own. In a very short time they had established an exchange and barter system, and in return for Trissie's pig swill, sympathy and breakfast, the Beresfords and their lodgers were getting bacon, pork, chicken, fresh vegetables and eggs. Tea and sympathy would also be turned into rations of eggs/bacon/vegetables for the washers-up, who would return the compliment with clothing coupons. As a system it was pretty fool-proof, until the day a WAAF friend turned up on forty-eight hours' leave. In exchange for board and lodging she gave Trissie a grey blanket which she had 'acquired' from her billet.

The ever practical Trissie was delighted and within a week the liberated blanket had been dyed navy blue, taken to the ancient local tailor, and transformed into an overcoat for Liza. As she had been wearing the same increasingly tight, shabby coat for three years she was really happy and wore it constantly. When there was a thunderous knock on the front door one night, she was still wearing it as she dived through the meshes of the blackout curtains to open the door.

Standing on the doorstep were two enormous Canadian military policemen. She knew instantly that they had traced her and the coat and shot downstairs to the basement kitchen where, yet again, patient Mr Thirkell was taking Trissie through her household accounts.

'It's the police,' Liza said in panic. 'It's the coat!'

'Put it under your mattress,' Trissie said crisply, 'and get into bed. They will never be allowed to search your room while I'm here!'

Mr Thirkell supported Trissie upstairs to confront the military. As everybody was rather confused it took some time for the MPs to get to the point. They were looking for Liza's brother Marcus. Apparently he had been overcome by a surge of patriotism after the fall of France, had abandoned Hollywood and crossed the 49th parallel to join the Canadian Army to fight in England, but he had gone under the wire again and quietly crossed back into the USA. He was now officially a deserter. The Canadian Army had come to the conclusion that in some magical way he had managed to cross the Atlantic and return to Brighton. As all this was news to Trissie, she was as flummoxed as the MPs.

'I'm sure you must be mistaken,' she said. 'Marcus has always hated the army. He didn't even like the OTC at school. Would you like to search the house? I must go and riddle the donkey,' by which she meant stoke the boiler. The military policemen stood silently contemplating the diminutive woman standing between them and their objective and then thought better of it and turned on their heels, fighting their way back out through the blackout curtains. They never heard from MPs again, but it was about a month before Liza dared to wear her coat.

Meanwhile, at Brighton & Hove High it soon became obvious that scholastically, the standard was far higher than anything Liza had yet encountered. Night after night she sat cross-legged in the small basement lumber room below stairs, trying to do homework and ignore a particularly unnerving device called the 'whistling' bomb.

> We weren't under continuous bombardment, we just seemed to get the strays which unloaded everything as they returned to their bases in France. It played havoc with our nerves and the lodgers congregated on the landing talking in high-pitched voices about nothing in particular. If the night got really noisy all twelve of us would shelter in the basement and to hell with homework.

It was a strange household for a 14-year-old girl to live in; there was no one else under the age of 60, but it gave Liza a great fund of anecdotes and characters to draw on in later life.

Their most prized lodger was an old friend of Trissie's, Mrs Mona Grenville. Aden referred to her as the 'first floor front', which meant that she paid more than anyone else for the best room in the house, five guineas a week, full board. She had once been a famous actress and a leading lady of Sir John Hare; when the air raids hotted up she would launch into Shakespeare:

> 'Once more into the breach...' whee, pause, thump, 'Once more' wheeee, pause, crash. Or 'close up the wall...' CRASH. 'Trissie dear, I think we had better go down to the basement.'

They were a pretty strange company in the faint, blue, basement light. Among the regulars were the Misses Thirkell, cousins of Mr Thirkell. He was in his mid-seventies but they were both well into their eighties and always, for some strange reason, wore hats at all times, even when thumping slowly upstairs to take a bath. They shared a bedroom, were utterly devoted to each other and belonged to a strict religious sect which had been started in the Midlands some 150 years previously. Their religion was very much a family affair and they were the last surviving grandchildren of the founder. When they went, it went. They didn't hold with smoking, drinking, or possibly sex as there was no younger generation and they talked a lot about the 'bottomless pit'. Aden used to egg them on to describe it, aided by Liza's favourite lodger, Miss Ford.

Miss Ford was always dashingly dressed, 1920s style. She looked immaculate, was sharp-tongued and, in her mid-sixties, was the youngest boarder. With her fringe, short hair bob and long cigarette holder she looked like something out of the movies. Her room, top floor front, was crammed with art nouveau furniture, paintings, pot plants, shawls and two enormous castor oil plants which she called Fred and Emily. She also had a cocktail cabinet and on the first of the month she would buy her rationed bottle of gin and weave into the dining room, ignoring the basilisk stare of the Miss Thirkells, sit down at her table with a thud, take a deep breath and then sing quite loudly and beautifully, 'I am Titania, Queen of the Fairies', while beating time with a knife. It was the cue for everybody to start talking as loudly as possible, but Miss Ford didn't give a damn and would carry on singing. Once she so mesmerised 85-year-old Alice that she forgot to move off the food lift which was creakingly wound up from the basement, bearing the puddings. To Alice's, and everyone else's surprise, she found herself rising several feet off the floor.

Miss Ford's nephew came to see her occasionally. He was very charming and polite and, to Trissies's delight, became an equerry at Buckingham Palace.

Their second favourite lodger was Mrs Scott who was plump, pretty, vague and getting more absent-minded by the day. She was a widow with a large family, including several handsome grandsons who were army captains and naval lieutenants and who somehow edged in on the extra meal rota system. Their youth and masculinity electrified the atmosphere to such an extent that the Misses Thirkell wore their best hats, Miss Ford offered round her precious de Reskie cigarettes with abandon, and old Alice, her corset creaking like pistol shots, always managed to get them second helpings.

The only lodger who wasn't affected by their presence was Miss Bishop, second floor front. She was the daughter of a Dean, the sister of a Canon, and even in advanced old age she still had the kind of face which made people say, 'She must have been beautiful as a girl.' She was like a statue, it was as though long ago something in her life had frozen her for ever. Her room was as tidy, cold and impassive as she was. Her manners were perfect, she kept everyone at arm's length and wore white cotton gloves to read *The Times* because the print was dirty. She lived a solitary life and during even the noisiest of raids she sat bolt upright in her deckchair in the dim, blue-lit basement reading the Bible.

In the second floor back was Miss Newman who had been a missionary in Japan for forty years. She somehow managed to exist on a tiny pension and was their lowest payer at £2-12s-6d a week. The love of her life was Japan and its people, regardless of the fact that England was now bitterly at war with them.

'They are such sweet, gentle people,' she said, 'they would never hurt anyone and the bathwater was always hot in Japan.'

'I wonder you didn't stay there,' said Miss Ford, fitting another de Reskie into a long holder, which earned her two filthy looks from the Misses Thirkell, 'since you loved it so much.'

Poor Miss Newman was bewildered, Mrs Scott went on getting into terrible trouble with her socks for sailors knitting, and Miss Butler kept on reading with pursed lips.

'I shall now recite some poetry,' said Aunt Mona [Grenville], rearranging her Angora shawl, 'If by Rudyard Kipling, one of our finest poets. Did I ever tell you about the time I first met him? It was when Sir John and I were on tour...'

They had all heard it fifty times but were too tired, indifferent, scared or polite to say so and the night would drift away until the blessed all-clear sounded and they could get back to their beds. The only person who seemed to be totally unaffected by the raids was Mr Thirkell who, being the only resident male, always put his clothes on over his pyjamas so as not to upset any sensibilities, and who spent most of his time in the basement trying to unravel Trissie's erratic bookkeeping.

Mrs Thompson, first floor back, never went down to the basement no matter what happened. She was the widow of a Canon, had travelled all over the world, mostly by yak according to her, and who spent much of her time twiddling the knob on her ancient wireless trying to find a church service. She only moved out of her room to have a bath or go down for meals; she always carried a Bible with her and propped it up against her pepper pot – and probably against the hot water tap in the bath too.

Finally there was Dr Bignold. She looked exactly like an elderly Queen Victoria with her receding chin and hair drawn back in a tight bun. She was very stout and wore enormous balloon-type dresses almost down to the ground. She was a highly qualified Doctor of Medicine, worked twelve hours a day in the Brighton Medical Centre and despised everyone except Trissie, whom she vaguely recognised as another working woman. Her one relaxation was keeping rabbits in the tiny back garden. She was very comforting as she took no notice at all of the air-raids or of anybody's aches and pains, which she always diagnosed as 'nonsense'. When Trissie sent Liza up to Miss Bignold's room, second floor back, with a crimson tongue, aching throat and burning ears, she examined her and said tersely, 'Pure imagination. Nothing wrong with you child. Go for a good long walk and then have two glasses of water.'

Liza may have had acute tonsillitis but such was the force of Dr Bignold's personality that she did exactly as she was told and recovered.

However, even Miss Bignold ('never call me doctor') had an Achilles heel – her beloved rabbits. Night after night she entered the dining room rubbing her hands and announcing, 'Saul's got diarrhoea again. I've dosed him but he's not well. Henrietta is carrying but Matthew's losing weight.' She had forgotten that she had intended fattening them up for the dinner table and instead, grown fond of them.

As Liza and the lodgers chomped their way through Woolton pie and apple pudding followed by half an ounce of cheese, they were given the grisly details until matters reached such a pitch that an emergency meeting was held in the sitting-room. The lodgers were unanimous, they could not eat Miss Bignold's rabbits.

As Trissie had been banking on the rabbits to see everyone through a few meals, it was a crisis. Her solution was simple and effective: she gave Miss Bignold's live rabbits to the butcher who gave her in exchange already butchered anonymous rabbits – or so she said. The result was that they all ate rabbit stew, curried rabbit and rabbit pasties happily, greedily, and with a clear conscience that they were not eating Miss Bignold's pampered pets. History does not relate whether she partook of the feast, but pragmatism probably won the day.

There was one thing which they all had in common regardless of sex or age; they were hungry. The great highlight of the week was Sunday lunch when somehow, come hell or Hitler, the household had trifle. The cake and the jam were ersatz, the custard was made with dried eggs (which smelt disgusting in its raw state), but on the top was cream, made by

Liza using an egg-whisk for about half an hour on the carefully hoarded tops of the milk. Topping this were decorations of more ersatz jam. One Sunday the spirit of revolt rose up in Liza as she whisked the milk on and on, and instead of adding the carefully hoarded jam to the trifle tops she used tomato chutney.

Trissie always served the portions of trifle to avoid any cheating.

'Not for me, thank you' said Liza, poised for instant flight. To her astonishment spoonful after spoonful of the hideous concoction was swallowed at high speed.

'Delicious' said Miss Bignold, glancing up momentarily from *Rabbits in Sickness and Health.* 'Absolutely delicious, Mrs Beresford.'

Trissie who fortunately had declined the trifle too, beamed and tried to look modest as Liza slumped off to the basement, her moment of revolt squashed. Aden was fascinated by this episode and it reinforced his belief that people rarely noticed anything. He determined to carry out an experiment to prove this. With the aid of two hairpins secretly purloined from Trissie, and with a great deal of fiddling, he took the precious cuckoo clock apart and switched round the bellows. When everybody was at their tables waiting hopefully for their supper at 7 o'clock, he said loudly:

'I think my watch has stopped. Has anyone got the right time?' All eyes swivelled to the clock, there was the familiar whirring sound and out came the cuckoo which paused for a second and the sang quite distinctly seven times:

'Oo-cuck, oo-cuck, oo-cuck...'

'Seven o'clock, dear' said Aunt Mona and there was a general murmur of assent.

Like all adolescents Liza was now leading a double life. Apart from her household duties, carrying up breakfast trays, shopping errands and clearing the gas meters every Saturday, and school, she had a third existence which was sneaking off to the cinema and theatre when she had saved enough pocket money and there was no chance of getting caught. The Theatre Royal was still open and putting on weekly plays prior to them going in to London, and for half a crown there was a seat in the gods to watch some of the very best actors. On Thursday afternoons, when she should have been playing hockey or doing prep, she clocked out of the basement after lunch, cycled off and crept up to the wooden seats with a greasy bag of whatever food she could lay her hands on. She often paid for tickets with purloined money from the gas meter, as she slid a few shillings here and there into her shoes.

We had quite a clique going up in the gods. Most of them very elderly who panted and creaked up the endless stone staircase, also carrying sandwiches. It was a very friendly club as we munched, gazed and munched. I was never caught and saw, and was entranced by, the very best actors, including a very young Richard Burton in *The Lady's Not For Burning*.

It was heady stuff and she loved the cinema too.

I came out of *Citizen Kane* and felt as if I were free-wheeling all the way home, the production was so extraordinary. But the best of all was *Gone With The Wind*. It took several weeks to raise the money for the extortionate ticket price of five shillings. With great care I wrote a lying note to the History Mistress to explain that I had to go and support the tennis team. I was so bad at tennis I was the only non-playing captain of the school, so it was chancy. So was playing tennis; we had been taught that if there was a sudden unexpected aerial fight we should put our rackets over our heads as a protection against shrapnel as we ran for cover.

But at this point there was a kind of retribution. Scarlet O'Hara was flirting away when the 'crump, crump, crump' started. The screen dimmed and a notice came up telling the audience that an air raid was in progress and that those wishing to leave their seats were cordially invited into the air raid shelter.

There was a patter, patter, patter on the cinema roof as Scarlet proclaimed that Rhett was 'nothing but a damn Yankee'. It wasn't a hard decision to make. Five shillings was a fortune so Liza saw the rest of the film from a nearly deserted row of seats, or, when the noise got really bad and there was shrapnel hitting the roof, she got down on her hands and knees and watched it on all fours from the side of the aisle. 'It gave the burning of Atlanta a whole new dimension but I did have to read the book again afterwards to catch up on a few gaps in the plot when I had my eyes shut.'

While Liza was Hollywood struck, Marcus had long since forsaken it. The family knew nothing about his whereabouts since the thwarted visit by the Canadian Military Police who had alerted them to the fact he had left California. Then one day he suddenly arrived on the front door step with a gingery beard, a very gaunt face and a battered suitcase of unspeakable clothes which were slimy and smelly.

'Cockroach eggs and maggots,' Marcus explained.

Trissie was horrified, begged him not to tell the lodgers and all his clothes were boiled while he slept round the clock. After abandoning the Canadian Army, he had joined the American Merchant Service and had been on one of the appalling convoys to Russia. When the convoy finally docked none of the crew were allowed ashore and heavily armed soldiers patrolled up and down the quay to make sure that no Allied foot touched Mother Russia. Subsequently, his ship was torpedoed.

He had acquired a strong American accent but lost it after about a week and spent most of his time sleeping in a tiny attic room (top floor front) and after all his experiences little hit-and-run raids meant nothing to him and he slept through them.

Being rather in awe of her gaunt, much-travelled brother, Liza didn't have the nerve to bring up a small financial matter. Some time previously when Marcus was in Hollywood Aden had received information (goodness know how) that Marcus had got into a little bit of trouble with the Mexican police. In fact, not to put too fine a point on it, he was in prison and very much wanted to get out again and this could be arranged for the very reasonable sum of £20.

Aden and Liza knew they couldn't tell Trissie, who would have had a fit, and it was no good approaching Tristram as he and Marcus, two powerful and highly intelligent personalities, had never exactly seen eye to eye about anything. Tristram had his family to support and was working at full stretch on his farm seven days a week to make ends meet. JD, now living in the West Country, was no longer selling well and Aden was equally hard up. As it happened, Liza had exactly £20 in the Westminster Bank. It was her Emergency Fund in case they got bombed again and it had been laboriously built up from occasional tips, birthday and Christmas money and, of course, a few purloined shillings from the gas meters.

Aden and Liza met after school in the bank. It was getting dark and there was a raid on.

'Excuse me, I wonder if we could talk to you privately,' Aden asked the ancient cashier who lent across the counter, hand to his ear.

'Speak up, please.'

All the bank staff were elderly and deaf and poor Aden had to end up shouting.

'It's about our brother who's in prison…'

Lucky for him there were no other customers as they had all taken shelter. They were finally beckoned down to the end of the counter. The cashier listened in astonishment and then, to their undying gratitude, he calmly unravelled the situation as though it were a common daily occurrence, agreed that something must be done as speedily as possible and somehow produced a document, got Liza to sign it, and that was it. They were bowed out between the sandbags with great politeness. Somehow the money was transferred to Mexico and Marcus was released – which is why Liza remained with the Westminster Bank, now the Natwest, for the rest of her life. If they could deal so competently and politely with a weird situation like that, she always felt that they could deal with anything. Much later, JD heard about Liza's sacrifice and insisted on sending her the £20. As he was more broke than ever, she was very touched by his kindness. Trissie remained in blissful ignorance.

It was now 1942 and Liza decided to join up and do her bit for the war effort. As she was 15 and 17½ was the minimum age for enlisting in the services there was a slight problem, but she was determined. One of the lodgers had left and her room was taken by an ATS officer. She was a major with a slightly erratic character who got on very well with Miss Ford. Part of the reason, although it wasn't apparent at the time, was that she could freely lay her hands on gin.

'The army is a very good life for girls,' she announced as she strode into the dining room in her immaculate uniform. As everybody else was considerably over the age of joining anything, even the Home Guard, this remark was obviously addressed to Liza and she absorbed it willingly. Apart from school, she was with old people constantly so the services seemed rather appealing. Wearing her dyed coat and Deanna Durbin hat, and a lot of secretly acquired lipstick surreptitiously applied after leaving home, Liza went to the recruiting office and gave her age as 17. It all seemed to go well and she expected to be enrolled, signed, sealed and delivered to a new exciting life.

However, the game was up two days later when the major's new driver, who also happened to work in the Recruiting Office, pushed the front door bell and, still in school uniform, Liza pounded up from the basement to answer it.

Shortly afterwards the major succumbed to the DTs and was taken away and never seen again. Life in the services was over. Or was it? Liza, with her best friend Pog, decided that half a uniform was better than none and they joined the Women's Junior Air Corps. As Liza had craftily given Trissie the idea that is was rather like being in the Girl Guides, she agreed that she should go off for two evenings a week to 'train' in a grim and draughty gym hall. There they drank very pale ersatz coffee and learned the rudiments of drill at the request of a charming officer who looked like a pretty pouter pigeon.

'Form threes or do I mean fours? Wait a moment while I look at the book. Oh dear, never mind, let's begin again. Pog, you'd better be marker, dear, if you don't mind…'

There was also a disillusioned RAF Sergeant who instructed them on the Morse Code.

We got quite good at it and reached the heights of being able to read and send at twelve words a minute. We got quite 'Morse happy' – you'd hear it everywhere – and we used to 'diddy-diddy-da-dit' to each other in school by tapping on our school desks, which understandably drove our teachers mad.

They were marched from the Gym Hall to the Metropole Hotel, which was a shadow of its former glamorous self as it was jammed with RAF cadets. They showed signs of wanting to be even more friendly than the Dutch/Czechs/Poles, but the girls' officer was having none of that and herded them into the former ballroom, converted into a classroom, where they were instructed in aircraft recognition.

'Now this is a Messerschmitt,' said their instructor, another world-weary RAF Sergeant. 'Notice the shape of the wings and the trailing ailerons …'. They did their best, but most of girls' attention was on the giggling RAF cadets who were segregated at the rear desks.

'And this is a Fockerwolf … I said *Focker*wolf, shut up at the rear…. ladies present, er, pardon me, madam, er captain, er miss….'

Liza enjoyed Aircraft Recognition and it came in useful one morning in Art Class as there was a sudden rattle of gunfire and two grey shapes scudded over the glass roof.

'One of ours,' said the unconcerned art mistress.

'No it isn't, Miss Brow,' said Pog, 'it's a Fockerwolf, note the shape of…'

A series of crump, crump, crump drowned her voice and as the class snatched up their drawing boards and clasped them over their heads as the windows shattered. As was the norm, the school alarm and the siren sounded simultaneously, rather late in the day, and minutes later there was the 'All Clear'. The whole school was summoned into Main Hall. The headmistress who was quite young and so dashing that she sometimes wore diamond earrings with her gown, looked pale and anxious.

'Some of you,' she said, 'may be a little upset when you go home at lunch time. Nevertheless I shall expect you all back in school this afternoon. Dismiss!'

Liza didn't think the remarks applied to her. Another of Liza's best friends, Smiler, lived in the same part of Brighton, about two miles from the school, and caught the same bus home for lunch. The bus was diverted and then diverted again; Liza got off at a barrier at the top of her road and told the warden where she lived. He gave her a strange look and beckoned her under the makeshift barrier. 'There was the horrible, familiar smell of dust everywhere and a nearby house had become a giant doll's house with its front missing. Our house had lost all its windows and the stonework was pock-marked with shrapnel. There was dust falling gently like summer rain.'

Luckily nobody was hurt. Like grey ghosts, Trissie, Liza and the lodgers all tried to eat their dried egg omelette and behave normally. Liza helped to sweep up some of the damage until it was time to catch the bus.

'You all right?' asked Smiler.

'Mmmm'

'You aren't wearing your beret, you'll lose marks.'

Nobody said anything about the missing beret and the headmistress sent for Liza, gave her a cup of tea and talked about work. She said Liza just wasn't pulling her weight at the school.

It was masterly psychology because I stopped feeling sick and became determined to show her what I could do, with the result that I became secretary of a variety of school societies until she sent for me again and gave me a short, sharp lesson on the virtues of delegation. She was a superb Head and we all adored her, especially when she produced an American Naval Captain as guest of honour at the prize-giving. He was unbelievably handsome and charming and we all fell instantly in love with him.

'Hey, isn't she something?' he said, grabbing our revered Head round her shapely waist. 'I think I'll have to give her a kiss…' and he did. She blushed and the entire school rose to their feet and roared approval. Some of the more elderly staff looked a bit sour but the gallant Captain with a bravery far above and beyond the call of duty insisted on kissing them too. Perhaps he'd been at sea rather a long time. It was the most riotous prize-giving ever and it did our jaded morale a power of good.

Somebody else to whom the Beresfords owed a lot was the well-known novelist, D.L. Murray, one of Brighton's brightest stars. He lived near the Beresfords and was a generous and larger-than-life personality who, out of the kindness of his heart, agreed to go and speak to the school Literary & Historical Society. It was a triumph to have captured him and everybody was in a twitter of nerves, even the sophisticated headmistress. The school front door bell rang and with clattering feet Liza went to welcome their distinguished guest. He gripped hold of her hands, his own like ice.

'Lizzy,' he said trembling, 'I'm terrified!'

Stage fright or not, he gave a brilliant talk on 'Humour' and reduced them all to tears of much needed laughter.

As if the small air raids weren't enough to keep the citizens of Brighton jittery, an enormous mine, bristling like a vast hedgehog, was washed up on a beach. Loudspeaker vans patrolled the streets telling people to leave their windows open as when it exploded they stood a good chance of losing their remaining windows. They obeyed but by the afternoon, which had turned grey and chilly, people had lost interest. Liza came home from school, boiled the kettle, made Trissie's tea and pounded upstairs with the tray to her bedroom, where she was having her much deserved afternoon nap. At the precise moment when Liza was about to put it on the bedside table, the mine blew up with a tremendous roar. The window was half open but, complete with curtains and frame, it detached itself and crashed over Liza who fell across her mother's bed, festooned with shattered glass, sticky tape and splintered wood. Somehow she managed not to spill a drop of the precious milk and tea. She did, however, give vent to her feelings.

'Jesus Ker-ist!' she shouted as the choking smother of dust and plant showered down.

Trissie shot up in bed, her face rigid with horror.

'Elisabeth, WHAT DID YOU SAY?' She brushed splintered glass and the remains of a picture out of her hair and off the bed.

'NEVER say that again! Do you understand? And pour out my tea. I'm extremely angry with you!'

Trissie could reluctantly come to terms with the war but she was not prepared to tolerate blasphemy.

Eventually, however, she needed all her resilience because at long last Liza achieved her ambition to join the services and signed on in 1944, this time legitimately, with the WRNS.

At the start it was rather like being back at boarding school because we didn't speak to one another and we were billeted in London, bewildered by this strange life where we had to learn a whole new vocabulary. Lavatories were ablutions, left and right became port and starboard and as we clattered up seven enormous flights of stone stairs at 6 am we were 'going aft', whatever that meant. We were issued with stiff, heavy uniforms, lisle stockings and creaking black shoes which always had to be highly polished. We were also issued with bedding and given the distinct impression that if we made up our bunks with the anchor on the cover facing the wrong way it would endanger the whole British fleet.

They were marched and counter marched and divided into two categories, either working in the kitchens (galleys) or on cleaning. Liza considered herself lucky to get allocated to cleaning which meant being called at 5.45 am and then slowly scrubbing down the vast flights of stone stairs while a pale spring moon slowly sank out of the sky. She loved every moment, particularly the quiet feeling of being alone in the world, as she sloshed away retreating step by step, while from time to time a Chief Petty Officer would come panting up and say 'Circular movement with the scrubbing brush. Not so much water. Rinse properly.' She was an ex-chambermaid from a big London hotel and wore white cotton gloves. Slowly and dramatically she would slide one fastidious finger underneath a step and if that finger got a smudge of dirt on it should would shake her neat auburn curls and Liza had to start cleaning again.

They were all given some mysterious tests which involved fitting together bits of odd-shaped jigsaws and were asked all kinds of random questions and maths problems very quickly.

'All right, you'll do,' the Inspecting Officer said. 'No need to go any further. Next!'

As a result Liza was transferred to another 'ship' nearer central London. It was a smaller, somewhat cosier establishment where a group of them underwent a crash course in Morse. Although she had a flying start with her twelve words a minute, she soon found herself very much in the rearguard and struggling hard. The ace girl in the class was an apple-cheeked 17½-year-old from Cornwall known by her initials, BJ.

BJ had never been away from Truro before but she took London in her stride, retained her lovely Cornish accent, and soon showed the Home Counties girls a clean pair of heels. She had an IQ of terrifyingly high proportions and within a couple of months of intensive training she was way ahead of their instructor. Another Wren with whom Liza became friends was Lily who was also bright, but looked like a startled hare and quite often wore her cap and her skirt back to front out of sheer nerves. They had a flagpole in the central courtyard and it was the job of the duty Wren to lower the flag when there was an air-raid. It was Lily's bad luck to be on duty when the siren and the all-clear sounded thirty-two times. She started off well enough but by the finish she was totally distraught and the flag, her cap and her lisle stockings were all at half-mast as she sagged against the pole. Their CO came roaring through the gates, paused and looked at Lily, who shut her eyes and waited to be keel-hauled at the very least.

'I think,' said the voice of the Establishment gently, 'that you'd better leave the flag down and get to your bunk.'

Another Wren, Joanna, was tiny, pink-cheeked with dark curly hair and always looked neat. She never had holes in her stockings, her uniform was immaculate and she attracted Americans/Canadians/Poles like bees to the honeypot. In order to give her some protection BJ, Lily and Liza formed a group round her as they ventured out to explore London in the blackout. It was just as well as the Americans showed every sign of being very friendly indeed, and in some mysterious way had an endless supply of shiny nylon stockings. An added safeguard was that they had to be back 'on board' by 10 pm, and Liza reckons there were many times when they must have been close to achieving a four-minute mile as they came out of the underground and pounded up the Finchley Road to get back on time. In peacetime their Establishment had been a theological college and a rumour soon circulated that one of the students had hung himself from the balcony in the very large, very gloomy library building at the back. Each night two of them were detailed off to the blackout and as they rattled round in the eerie twilight they did our best to frighten each other to death. Then one night something sinister occurred.

BJ, Lilly, Joanna and Liza shared the top bedroom. They were lying on their bunks dit-dahing to each other as Liza vacantly gazed out of the small window at what seemed to be a low-flying shooting star.

'It's very pretty,' she said. 'Oh! It's gone!'

There were a few seconds' silence and then a bang which made the windows rattle.

'There's another, and another and ANOTHER! I say, do come and look!'

More silence, then a crescendo of explosions.

'BJ, do come and see…'

Nobody answered and Liza turned round to find that her cabin-mates had to taken to their heels and were halfway to the shelter.

It was a weird night, because none of us knew what was happening. First there was this strange clattering noise, then silence and finally a tremendous bang. We were sleeping three to two mattresses, head to toes and heaven help you if your next door sleeping partner hadn't washed her feet recently. I dozed uneasily and there was a strange atmosphere about our 'ship' the next day. Lily said that she had heard it from the Head Cook that it was the Germans who had landed in Sussex and they were firing on us from there. In a panic I tried to ring Mother, imagining her and all the lodgers being taken prisoner in the basement and marched off to prison camp. But there were 'no calls' to the South Coast and my imagination went mad.

Slowly, the real truth leaked out. This was the German's new secret weapon, the VI or buzz-bomb. The engine cut out for some seconds and then it exploded. Gradually they adapted to it.

The great thing about it was that it gave you a sporting chance because you could follow its laboured progress and when the engine cut out you dived for cover and started counting. If you got to 10 then you knew you were ok. On the other hand, there was no siren to give you prior warning. I was at the underground station when one came droning overhead. There wasn't another soul in sight. I crouched down on all fours and put up one hand to slide the fare money to an invisible clerk. Another hand appeared, scooped it up and issued a ticket and then both of us fell flat on our faces and began to intone 'one, two, three…' We never did meet face to face.

I was in the middle of a large department store when there was a familiar drone followed by silence. I looked round and there wasn't another person to be seen. Not a customer or an assistant. It was all mine and for one mad moment I imagined scooping up everything in sight. Instead I got down into the familiar crouching position on all fours, hands clasped behind the head and began to count.…

All through the daylight hours people whose houses had been hit trudged past the 'ship' pushing prams, wheelbarrows and bicycles festooned with all their worldly possessions.

It was a sad procession and had the air of a sinking ship. One doodlebug came down uncomfortably close just as we were halfway through lunch. Everybody dived under the table and there was the familiar 'whoosh' as chanting in unison we reached 'two-three-four' when in came the windows with the familiar crash of splintering glass and we clambered upright coughing and flapping our hands.

The chief cook, a fiery character from Yorkshire who stood no nonsense from anyone, not even the Commanding Officer, came banging in from the galley, hands on hips and surveyed the shambles dispassionately. 'The boogers have ruined my pud!'

Just as they were learning to live with the doodlebugs, the V2s started.

They really did scare us, because they gave no warning at all, they just exploded. I was walking up towards Charing Cross Road when one of these monsters suddenly exploded far too close for comfort. I grabbed at the plinth of the Edith Cavell statue, my nose buried against the cold stone. Both of us survived and I've had a soft spot for her ever since. The words on the plinth are carved into my memory: *Patriotism is not enough. There must be no bitterness in my heart.*

After the Normandy landings the pressure on the new WRNS to learn wireless operating skills increased even more.

We began to look like a group of white mice with insomnia. We heard Morse everywhere: in the clatter of knives on plates, the creaking of a window, the patter of footsteps. We had become known as 'diddy-dah happy', and even BJ began to lose her sunny good temper and some of her high standards as instead of meticulously darning her stockings she, like the rest of us, merely blacked in the relevant pieces of leg with ink so that the holes wouldn't show. Lily began talking in her sleep and if one of us snapped at her she would start running round the cabin (bedroom) like a demented March hare. I merely talked to myself under my breath all the time, which drove the others even more demented.

Instead of getting better at work, we regressed with alarming speed into fits of amnesia, usually followed by tears. Then, one night a VI clattered towards us and cut out. There was instant silence from all of us.

'Take cover!' I shouted. They already had and it served me right because I was in a top bunk that night – a great luxury compared to sharing a mattress – and I received a chunk of plaster in my mouth on the word 'cover'. A large number of girls were on leave that weekend and when the rest of us surveyed our ship in the morning our officers must have given thanks because if there had been a full complement it would have been a disaster. As it was we were about 'half sunk' but nobody was hurt.

We four surveyed the damage on our deck and having been given the order to clear up and make it ship-shape as best we could, we were issued with brooms and dustbins. We held our own muttered council of war. 'We can't wear uniform,' said Joanna, 'It'll get torn and filthy.'

'I suppose we could just wear our underwear,' suggested Lily. BJ, a true puritan, turned this down instantly. When it was her turn to have a six-inch bath, she always got undressed underneath her dressing-gown. Liza had a brainwave.

'We'll wear our uniforms with nightdresses on top. I'll lend you mine.'

At last the despised school nightdresses had come into their own and, looking rather bulky, they started to clear up what they could. By unanimous vote they had decided not to wear their caps as well, as four stout 17-year-olds wearing pink cotton nighties over skirts, shirts and coats, looked funny enough already.

They were busily sweeping and cleaning when down the wrecked companion-way (corridor) came the sound of feet and voices. They stopped working and gazed at each other in an agony of indecision. Nothing in King's Regulations and Admiralty Instructions told them what to do in a situation like this. They couldn't salute as they had no caps on. Into view swept an imposing cavalcade of the very top brass, with blue rings practically up to their elbows, immaculate cocked hats, shiny shoes and rows and rows of ribbons. The four Wrens fell into line, brooms straight and gazed steadily ahead waiting for the axe to fall as their CO strode forwards. They were beyond grasping what she was saying until a very, very important officer swam into their terrified vision.

She held out an immaculately gloved hand and shook each of their filthy ones in turn: 'Well done, well done...'

She knew each of their names and to their further astonishment they saw that her eyes were full of tears. It was the Head of the Service, Dame Vera Laughton-Matthews.

'She was crying,' said BJ afterwards. 'Poor soul, I wonder why.'

They were all given emergency leave and issued with travel warrants. Liza felt as though she had been away for years as the train chugged across Sussex, and as the unchanging Downs rolled towards her she felt suddenly terribly homesick. Trissie, who was still hardly speaking to her as she didn't approve of women in uniform let alone women who wore trousers, nevertheless pulled out every stop as far as coupons were concerned. Unable to resist the steady roar of the sea, Liza went to lean on the railings of the top parade. She loved the sea and swimming and, next to cheese, she missed it most of all. A shadowy figure came to lean on the rail beside her, and in the moonlight she recognised a family friend whom she had known since childhood. At 19, he was a little older than her. They exchanged news and then he propped his elbows between the strands of barbed wire and she felt really proud to be alone with an RAF hero who had the DFC and Bar, and who was also very good looking. He was a member of the elite Path Finders.

He was shot down two months later.

Joanna, Lily, BJ and Liza were posted north and billeted in a seaside town on the Yorkshire coast. Their new 'ship' was a very old hotel which had been shelled in the First War and which, according to rumour, hadn't been lived in since. They were paid 'sixpence' for every bug they could catch. The bugs were small and fat, and having lived undisturbed were easy to capture. The women rapped their knuckles on the wall, holding out a matchbox, and into the box they fell. It was quite a lucrative sideline as their navy pay was (the equivalent of) 87p a week and Liza was paying 12p of that to her mother.

It was like being posted to a foreign land where the war had left the locals relatively unscathed: no bombs, no machine gunning, no VIs or V2s. These facts of life were brought home to the girls when BJ and Liza were walking down the main street. Suddenly there was a tremendous bang and they automatically fell onto their haunches, hands locked behind their necks to protect themselves from shrapnel. It was a passing truck back-firing. Everybody gaped at them and, with scarlet-faces, they got up and moved away at the double.

They were back on the Morse conveyor belt and with the peaceful nights and bracing sea air having a soothing effect, their speeds began to pick up. So did their social life as the town was packed with RAF officer cadets and it was nothing for one of the girls to get engaged, disengaged, and then engaged to a 'second fiancé' over one weekend.

Liza was inspired to write a 'murder with music' called *Toxine in Her Toddy*. It had a cast of eight and the high point as far as she was concerned was wearing a borrowed evening dress, held together at the back with safety pins while she sang *Jenny* in a light soprano. They played to a packed house of twelve, including the galley staff who would go anywhere as long as they could sit down for a bit. Joanna was the heroine, Lily the murderer, and BJ, wearing a moustache which kept coming unstuck ('Bless me, 'tis off again!') was the detective. It was Liza's first attempt at writing a script.

On one occasion, Liza was caught trying to climb in through a basement window long after lights out, but it was too late for court martial as they had all taken their passing-out exams, with BJ far in the lead with an almost unbelievable speed of twenty-eight words a minute – very fast indeed. They were posted south to HMS *Flowerdown*, in Hampshire. Operating as Admiralty 'Y' station, it was mainly responsible for intercepting Italian and Japanese naval communications, but also high frequency German, French and Russian Morse. Intercepts were sent on to Bletchley Park for intelligence assessment.

It was a large, sprawling, mixed camp and the four girls, sticking firmly together, were detailed to a Nissen hut with four others. They had four double bunks grouped round an evil-smelling but very necessary stove which grumbled and crackled day and night. It not only warmed them but there was always a slow-boiling kettle on the top. It just about dried their laundry and could be coaxed into making toast. The toast smelt of coke but no one cared, they were always hungry.

Those who were on Early Watch were woken by a sadistic sailor who marched round the outside of the hut holding a stick which rattled like hailstones on the tin walls, shouting 'Wakey, wakey'. Sometimes he thundered straight through the hut, giving the stove a vicious swipe en route. Either way he woke everybody up, including the girls who had come off late watch and were vainly trying to learn how to sleep in the daylight hours.

Compared to the sailors who were working a three-watch system, the Wrens worked four. The one they hated the most was going to bed in mid-afternoon and getting up at 11.30 pm with pasty faces and hooded eyes, a mug, knife, fork and spoon. One fateful night 'tea' consisted of fried bread and baked beans which were distinctly off. In spite of eternal hunger pangs the girls resisted and made do with slabs of bread and pale cocoa. At about 2 am, always the lowest ebb, disaster struck in the watch room and a large, previously healthy and able-bodied sailor, fell like an axed tree; he was followed by several more in all directions – all were suffering from food poisoning. The Chief Petty Officer in charge and the Night Watch Officer hauled out almost the entire male complement, who were incapable of carrying on at their listening posts; the rest of the watch found themselves doing treble duty. Fifty years later, while living on Alderney, Liza wrote:

The way to a man's heart may be through his stomach but that night we also learnt that it's a terrible sabotage route as well. Even now on a stormy night I find myself pulling the blanket over my head and saying fervently, 'thank God I'm not on watch tonight'. Occasionally, when it was a quiet watch, we were allowed a bit of time off which is when I learnt to go to sleep on a coke pile. The smell is bad but you get used to it. On the other hand it was pure bliss to come off watch at midnight from deep underground and into the dark, sweet, soft smell of the countryside with the nightingales singing as we stumbled back to the hut. But best of all was finishing at 8 am with a whole glorious thirty-four hours of freedom. Bleary-eyed breakfast was followed by a few hours' sleep then the world was our oyster and we made full use of it by hitch-hiking everywhere. Carefully travelling in pairs we criss-crossed the south of England. People were very good about giving us lifts, including on one occasion with an undertaker. We sat on the coffin in the back but luckily it was unoccupied at the time.

As their weekly pay was about a £1, public transport was out of the question, apart from the monthly travel warrant, so they continued to hitchhike during daylight hours. They thumbed down a fire engine, a general in his staff car which roared through the country lane at 80 mph; they rattled around in the backs of lorries, squeezed into already crowded

Austin Sevens, and even rode double pillion on the back of a motor bike. They were propositioned by three geriatric furniture removers who kept urging them to, 'Come up aloft and see the little room we've made over the driving cab. It's ever so cosy like....'

It was a running fight all the way to London but there were no hard feelings at the end of it. They were dropped off at Rainbow Corner, Piccadilly, where for a mere five shillings you could stay in youth hostels or YWCAs. As they learned the ropes their horizons widened and on four-day passes managed to get as far as Oxford, Truro and North Wales. They explored cathedrals (no entrance fee) and when they were lucky enough to pick up free Forces tickets, they went to the theatre. It didn't matter what the play was, they saw it for nothing.

There were occasional mishaps such as the night Liza went 'under the wire' for a rendezvous with a dashing American captain who was on a shore-based ship. Everyone in the hut had contributed something, so she was wearing Joanna's best shirt and tie, BJ's No 1 jacket and cap, her own skirt and stockings and Lily's shoes. She seemed all set for a glamorous evening which was to start with a cocktail party.

'I'm other ranks,' Liza nervously reminded her escort.

'Don't worry about a thing, honey. It'll all be fine.'

Other Rank 93252 polished Lily's shoes on the back of her stockings, her eyes dazzled after the dark as she entered a brightly lit room which was stiff with gold braid, tailor-made uniforms and tricorn hats. Quite suddenly an all too familiar face came into focus and she found myself gazing at her CO.

'And this is Other Ranks, Beresford,' said her escort beaming. The temperature dropped considerably. The CO knew very well that Liza had no right to be there and that technically she was a deserter.

'Oh really?' she said. 'How do you do?' She sent for Liza the next day, delivered a short, sharp lecture but didn't put her on a charge. After that they all became very much more circumspect about going under the wire, which meant getting their escorts to case the joint for top brass before the girls crept in after them.

On one occasion, Liza and BJ hitchhiked to Scotland and back for a £1.10s bet. By hitching everything that moved, they steadily travelled north, at one point crossing Carlisle on the back of a coal lorry in the rain. Once over the border they made for Edinburgh, a city which had shrugged off its wartime shabbiness with elegant disdain.

BJ and Liza, holding each other up, their eyes bloodshot with lack of sleep, homed in on the YWCA and although the sight of the wire mattresses and squared blankets were like a siren song, they forced themselves to ignore them. Somehow they had to prove that they had actually got there and the answer was two free tickets – they kept the stubs – for *Night Must Fall*. They nearly fell asleep but the resilience of being 18 and watching a terrifyingly gripping play worked wonders. They were just as lucky with hitchhiking on the way south and they won their bet.

Next to food, sleep was their second priority.

I owe an undying gratitude to the Service that it taught me to sleep under any conditions at a moment's notice. One night about 2 am, time of the lowest ebb when your mind and body are just about ticking over, I distinguished myself by falling asleep while walking up and down in a vain effort to keep awake. It was a very quiet uneventful watch with hardly a signal from the enemy radio stations we were monitoring. No air-raids, no U-boats surfacing – you had to be very fast to get a fix on their position as they were never above the sea for more than two minutes – when I was suddenly throttled. Not by by the CPO on duty but by my headphones. I had gone to sleep on my feet.

Their ship's company was now outnumbered about two-and-a-half to one by the Americans who were not only over here, over paid and oversexed – according to popular folklore – but who were all pretty overpowering. Most of the British male fellow watch-keepers had been on active service and then drafted to the land-based ship as a rest cure. They did not talk about what had happened to them, but they seemed to work a lot of it out of their systems in fights outside the pubs at closing time. But during the winter of 1944 and the spring of 1945 the atmosphere changed when the American troops were drafted across the Channel. They lost some of their dashing confidence and became homesick young men who talked endlessly about the girls and families they had left so far behind them.

Liza's 'ship' became more and more short-handed and their workload increased until the blue-lit watch room crackled with drama. Many years later, Liza wrote:

> Some of it remains with me still. Men died because of us and it remains with you forever. One night I was taking down immaculate four-letter word code when it faltered, paused and I picked up 'Heil Hitler, Heil...' and silence. The German sender was probably shot. It was strangely unreal emerging from below ground and into the normal world.

Then, quite suddenly, it seemed as if war in Europe was over. Chinks of light appeared in doorways and windows. Their work changed into new channels and they struggled to learn new and complicated techniques. Liza forged a letter purporting to be from Trissie which said that she would be delighted for Liza to serve overseas. Just as her posting to Ceylon came through the atom bomb was dropped and the war in Asia was over too.

> BJ and I were fortunate enough to have a weekend pass at the same time and we came trudging off watch only to discover that the kitchens had closed down for some inscrutable reason. We later discovered that double if not treble issues of rum had been doled out all round. For sheer knock-out potions I can recommend Navy rum on an empty stomach after a hard midnight watch, which may explain why we hitched a lift on a fire engine with BJ cleaning the bell like a lunatic while I clung to a shaft of pipe.

Some time later they found themselves in a London which had gone completely mad on VJ Night. The Free French were getting freer by the minute and were linking arms with the US Marines, Air Force and Army and were chasing all the women's services. There were Forces everywhere, wave after wave of them dancing down Whitehall, climbing the Cenotaph and surging up the Mall, singing and shouting and exchanging caps.

> It was all rather too much for BJ and me. We were suffering not so much from VJ night euphoria as hunger. If Lawrence Olivier

himself had asked us to join the knees-up in the middle of Whitehall we would have exchanged him for a packet of biscuits. We hadn't eaten for thirty-six hours and we were ravenous and desperate. We hammered on the door of a small bread shop. It was reluctantly opened a few inches. I stuck my foot in the gap and BJ surged in and grabbed a cake. We left a shilling on the counter and ran for it. We hacked it in half with my penknife and ate it sitting on the pavement outside the House of Commons.

Then with a few thousand other troops we surged towards Buckingham Palace as if drawn by a magnet. BJ and I scrambled up the Victoria monument in front of it and arms linked with other climbers we roared, *Two, four, six, eight, who do we appreciate? G-E-O-R-G-E, GEORGE!*

The massed crowd went mad when the Royal Family came out onto the balcony. They seemed as overcome as we were as we cheered our hearts out, throwing our caps in the air. I became on very friendly terms with a young Pilot Officer wedged next to me. He was handsome and charming but far more important, he was nursing a large, greasy pocketful of chips and he had a small two-seater open car. He eventually deposited two very tired ratings at Golders Green and the house of a very surprised aunt, Trissie's younger sister Dorothy. We slept blissfully on the floor and hitched back just in time for the first watch the next day.

A strange half life settled over the Wrens. It was a neither/nor period: there was still work to do but they couldn't get up any enthusiasm for it. The drive, the urgency, had gone out of them and having lived under conditions of pressure which would have turned a trades' union leader white overnight, they began to sag like old elastic. New and much more sophisticated equipment was being experimented with – the computer.

Liza started to write a very dramatic thriller on her log sheets. Page after page was passed round in the blue flickering light of the midnight watches. She would reach the end of a page and it would be snatched away. Everybody, even the toughest and most hard-bitten old rating, wanted to be in it, even if it was only a walk-on part. The book became stuffed with characters and she completely lost the plot but nobody cared as they grumbled their way through the tedium of the long nights.

'Roll on my demob' was the familiar cry, but it was 'last in, last out' and as BJ and Liza were the youngest and newest service girls, their return to civilian life still seemed lost in the hazy future. The hazier the better as far as Liza was concerned. Having tasted the heady wine of freedom, she dreaded what lay ahead. In the WRNS, the food, the living conditions, the hours of work had all been bad but she had made dozens of friends, been fascinated by her job and, as long as they had been on watch on time, they had been pretty free to come and go as they pleased. Her companions had been her own age and the thought of returning to all the old ladies and the slow pace of boarding house life was not a happy one. No more hitching lifts on the back of motor bikes or going to noisy camp dances; no more free travel round the countryside; no more being outnumbered by three to one so that even the plainest girl was never without a boyfriend.

One after the other the crew vanished into civilian life, their places being taken by earnest young boffins who weren't half as much fun. The washing lines which had once been hung with damp bellbottoms with an upside down bucket firmly wedged at the bottom of the legs to make them 'bell' more, so that when the wearer was out on the town their trousers swirled round them, now held pale utility shirts. No longer was 'make do and mend' piped over the loudspeakers to call the wearing watch-keepers from their bunks so that they could unroll their brown and white 'hussifs' (housewives – a kind of cotton sewing kit). A kind of male, piratical glamour was vanishing daily and in its place was the new, pale, tedious bureaucrat. Liza's naval career was coming to an end.

Chapter 3

A Wordsmith is Forged

It was 1946 when Liza found that the Admiralty was ready to dispense with her services and the ship's company was briskly deposited overboard into the chilly seas of civilian life. The four friends dispersed as they were shunted out into a brave new world at the ripe old age of 19, and clutching her £20 gratuity, Liza rejoined Trissie at the boarding house in Kemp Town. It was quite a jolt but Liza found she had swapped one commanding officer for another.

'Shorthand and typing,' Trissie ordered firmly, 'that's what you are going to do!' So, of course, she did.

The government paid for Liza to go to a secretarial college for 5½ months maximum, and paid her two pounds ten shillings a week for doing so. Liza remembered it as an awful Dickensian place, run by a true Victorian work master who strode up and down the lines of male and female pupils with a ruler in his hand. If they weren't going fast enough on 'the lazy dog jumps over', or 'now is the time for all good men…', whack! down came the ruler on their knuckles. As there were millions of ex-service people pouring onto the jobs market and work was as rare as clothing coupons, they put up with it.

The war was won and it was 'peace in our time' but it didn't feel like it as it was one of the coldest winters on record. From the third week of January to mid-March 1947, the whole country was frozen and lay under deep snow; thousands of livestock died, fuel was restricted, radio was limited and the nascent television service was suspended. Liza and her fellow trainees clumped to class wearing bits and pieces of odd, assorted uniforms topped by great coats and Air Force blue, Army Khaki and Navy blue. Some of the men wore balaclavas giving the impression of shabby refugees. At home Trissie started wearing her overcoat indoors and the old ladies were muffled up to the eyebrows; gas and electricity were low and often cut off as there was a fuel shortage.

Then they got the news that JD had had a stroke. Still under Trissie's injunction not to see her father, Liza told her that she was going to stay with friends and set off to go and see JD, who was living near Bath. She got half way to the West Country until the road was blocked by an impassable snowdrift and she was forced to return home. She never saw him again as he died shortly after. She always wished that she had known him better but was touched by his testamentary humour: he was extremely hard-up and he left each of his sons £288.18s.10d, but Liza was left £288.18s.11d as JD felt that as a girl she might need the extra penny. He had written to Liza secretly over the years and she had to get up early to waylay the postman so no one else should find out. But Trissie did find out, because when Liza returned from honeymoon in 1949 she found her old room in Brighton had been searched, the letters were discovered and had been burned in the kitchen boiler.

The boarding house survived the long winter of 1947. In the spring, Liza left secretarial college with an unreliable 120 wpm in shorthand, some knowledge of bookkeeping and a fast, inconsistent typing speed, but her spelling – a victim of her erratic schooling – remained uncorrected. It was time to find a job and Aunt Mona, their ground-floor-front lodger, who was now so frail Liza used to take in her early morning tea with her heart in her mouth in case she had died overnight, managed to arrange two interviews for her through connections. The first was with Conservative Central Office, then in a very large Victorian building in Victoria Street; the second was with the Foreign Office in Whitehall. The CCO was the nearer to the station, so Liza went there first. For her interview she wore her 'best' blouse, which was third-hand and still had a pre-war Jaeger label, her Wren skirt and greatcoat – naval buttons removed – Wren shoes, and her only pair of nylons. She was neat, respectable and terrified.

The Head of Personnel was an imposing lady who jutted straight out at the front like a shelf. The shelf was covered in crumbs and while she was interviewing me she kept dusting it down with little flicks of a dainty handkerchief. When she was satisfied that it was clean, she lent forward, opened the bottom drawer of her desk, took out a cake and began to eat it. More crumbs fell like the gentle rain from heaven until the cake was finished and it was dusting time again. I was so fascinated by this performance that I answered all her questions at random and after ten minutes I found I'd been taken on for three months' trial as a shorthand typist in the Publishing Department at three guineas a week.

In today's terms, the department would probably have been called Publicity and Public Relations. Liza abandoned all thoughts of the Foreign Office, which was probably just as well.

At first she had three bosses at Conservative Central Office. Mr Bunshot who was small, round, rosy and due for retirement. He spent all his time locked away in his cosy little office making long, confidential telephone calls to all the contacts he'd made during his years with the CCO. This was because he was planning to set up his own business and he firmly intended to take all his contacts with him. All he asked of Liza was to light his coal fire, dust his desk and answer his phone during his very long lunch hours. He never appeared to do any actual work at all.

Next in line was Mr Franklyn, a sad, dreamy man who was always immaculately dressed and who spent his time slowly rocking backwards and forwards on suede shoes as he gazed out of the windows. He would occasionally dictate a memo or two, pausing between each word which suited her unreliable shorthand, and would then forget all about them, so that after she had stopped putting the carbon in the wrong way round and used the rubber so much the paper looked like lacework, he would gaze at her mournfully and then go rocking off to his club without initialling any of them. There was something very strange about Mr Franklyn and it was months before it finally dawned on her that he was never, ever sober.

The third boss was Mr Woodham, known throughout the department as Woody. He was to alter the whole course of Liza's life.

He was tall, dark haired and in his fifties. His brown suits were always buttoned up wrongly and covered in dog hairs and he wore his tie under one ear and his spectacles were held together by darning wool so that one side was higher than the other, and he called everyone George regardless of their sex. For the first week, as I sat trembling behind my desk, he pounded through the office glaring at me ferociously. He terrified me and it wasn't until years later that he told me he was equally terrified of me as he'd never had a 'sekertery' before.

At the the start of the second week he put his head round the door and barked, 'Hey, you, come and take a letter.' Clutching her almost unused notebook in shaking fingers she dithered into his office. His desk was piled high to a depth of about nine inches with papers.

'Sit down, Miss-er-Miss.'

She sat, pencil poised. One thing she was sure of was that she could write 'Dear Sir' as fast as anybody in the business. Woody's glare became even more pronounced as he suddenly roared, 'George you miserable old devil you...'

And away he rattled. It was hopeless. By the time Liza had recovered from the shock and written a shorthand outline for 'George', he was on to his second paragraph. She scribbled furiously but the game was up and when he asked her to read her notes back she started to sniff and gulp. He whisked her notebook out of her hand and growled.

'I can't read this.'

'Neither can I.'

There was a long pause while he took off his crooked specs and cleaned them on his tie.

'Well, we'll 'ave to start again then, won't we? Now go and get me a cup of coffee, blow your nose and 'op it.'

They did start again, and yet again, but it was obvious to both of them that his shorthand and typing were infinitely superior. Lighting fires, dusting desks, emptying wastepaper baskets, getting cups of coffee and answering the phone was about Liza's limit. Doing very slow memos she could manage, but she was miles out of her depth trying to keep up with Woody who, although third boss in the pecking order, was actually running the whole department.

The crunch came on the day when she not only typed but sent a letter which said 'Dead Sir'. The recipient, an MP, was livid. He and Woody had a furious argument and Liza expected to lose her hitherto short-term employment at Conservative Central Office when Woody summoned her to his office. They stared at each other. They both knew that she was not up to the job and Liza waited for the axe to fall. But despite having been a tough war correspondent, Woody had a heart of pure marshmallow and was the kindest and most vulnerable of people.

'Well you're JD's daughter,' he growled, 'and I always did admire your father's work. Let's see if you can write. I'll think of something to tell Personnel, don't you worry, sweetheart. Now, let's start this letter again.'

The following Monday a very small, smartly dressed young woman with neat dark curls and piercing brown eyes joined the team. This was Miss Gridley, the new Senior Secretary.

She was a dynamo of efficiency; her pencil flew across the notebook, the carriage of her typewriter practically sent out sparks. She stood no nonsense from anybody. It was exhausting but exhilarating and the whole department seemed to come to life and from being a backwater, they moved to the front. The Chief Press Officer was in and out; the elegant Head of the Department paid them visits and even Lord Woolton, the party Chairman, came and beamed at them. But Woody knew, and so did Liza, that she was just about hanging on.

One Monday morning, in on time and at her desk, fires lit, everything dusted, Liza shot to her feet as Miss Gridley entered, immaculate as ever without a curl out of place. She shook out her umbrella, leant it against the wall and then put her hands on hips and to Liza's open-mouthed astonishment danced across the office singing:

> If a man's love is mighty
> He'll even buy a nightie
> For a girl that he thinks is fun…

Liza couldn't believe it. The staid, the super-efficient, the amazing Miss Gridley was dancing and singing at the top of her voice. Liza was transfixed.

Miss Gridley kicked off her size two gumboots and sank down at her desk.

'Now then, that's better,' she said breathlessly, while Liza continued to gaze at her like a stunned rabbit. 'First of all STOP calling me Miss Gridley, it makes me feel like Methuselah's mother. Call me "Gladdie".'

She also gave Liza good advice: 'Stop getting in such a panic about everything. Your shorthand, typing and filing aren't very good but they are a darn sight better than a lot of the butterflies in this department can do.'

The department had a large complement of debutantes who were always taking time off for parties, the hairdresser and sometimes Buckingham Palace.

'Stand up for yourself, Lizzie!'

It was the story of Liza's life but if you've been conditioned into being a doormat, it's extremely difficult to become a militant doormat overnight. Gladdie obviously recognised this and discussed it with Woody. The upshot was that Liza soon found herself working as a ghost-writer on the house magazine, a moribund journal of astonishing dullness.

'I can't write everything, miss,' said Woody. "Ere, you go and interview this old buzzard. Get 'er to tell you what frocks she wears and what she cooks her old man for his supper and whatever else you do, spell 'er name and title right!'

Which is how Liza became a reporter and learned to write for her living.

I wrote – to my utter astonishment and terror – ghost speeches for overworked MPs. Of course Woody double checked anything remotely important and added his own inimitable touches to personalise it for them. Reading 'myself' in Hansard was a bit unnerving and many years later I became friends with a real charmer, a long-retired cabinet minister [John Profumo] who fondly remembered my work and always called me 'Young Beresford'. He was so good looking we all used to buckle at the knees when he came in to see Woody.

Conservative Central Office still expected her to fulfil all the usual shorthand and typist duties, so with freelance payments as well she was now on a lordly eight guineas a week. The quarterly season ticket from Brighton to London was around the £5-6 mark, and she had to pay her mother for board and lodging so she got by very well.

All my spare cash went on clothes, mainly hats as they didn't need clothing coupons. Fenwicks in Bond Street was my favourite shop and the girls all called me by name and old Mr Fenwick himself turned up once to take a look at me. Heady stuff.

On the whole the CCO had a high dress standard. There were a lot of elegant and not-so-young men who always wore beautiful suits with a rosebud in their buttonholes, bowler hats, exquisitely-polished bespoke shoes and, regardless of the weather, carried a rolled umbrella. It seemed to Liza that they had all been at school/university/in the Guards,

Hussars or Green Jackets together. They were often related to 'Super Boss' as the Head of Department was known. He had a flat in Eaton Square, a house in Ireland – where he hunted – and his photograph was often in *The Tatler*.

He terrified me so much that on one occasion, when there was nobody else in the office – it was a Royal Garden Party day – he roared at me to take dictation. I became even more idiotic than usual. At the end of ten terrible minutes, Super Boss, his face the colour of his button holes, slammed both fists down on his desk and sent everything flying. He then kicked the wastepaper basket round the room until it ricocheted out of the door. His senior secretary, who had just returned from the Palace, calmly locked herself into the loo to repair her make-up.

'Come out!' He roared, shaking the handle and kicking the door so violently that some ancient plaster drifted down from the ceiling. I crouched down at my desk with my hands over my ears and my tears dripping onto my even more undecipherable shorthand. Super Boss's bull-like roaring was suddenly drowned by Woody's answering roar. The voices rose to a crescendo which was stopped in mid-blast by a cool, icy, deafening,

'Stop that AT ONCE!'

It was Gladdie, back from the Roneo department. She told Super Boss and Woody singularly and together what she thought of them, the department, the CCO and finally the male sex in general. She then hauled me out, dried my shorthand notebook and somehow made sense of the notes. The next day both of us received large bouquets from Super Boss, and Woody gave me a box of chocolates which he ate while he aired his views on the department.

Like Liza's mother, Woody had honed his prejudices down to a razor sharpness with which he demolished pomposity, stupidity, snobbishness, the bullying of half-witted shorthand typists, men who wore roses and the class war. Although his attitude to the latter was somewhat ambivalent as he tended to change sides according to the company he was in.

While he was in full flood, Super Boss put his bland face round the door and said, 'Care for a drink, Bill?'

'Well I wouldn't mind,' said Woody, kicking all his prejudices under the carpet. 'See you tomorrow, George. Glad you liked the chocolates.'

Gladdie and Liza united to protect Woody from the smooth machinations of Super Boss and all his elegant underlings. Woody was used quite shamelessly as he had an enormous talent and capacity for hard work, quite often putting in a twelve-hour day. He was the backbone of the whole department and they knew it, but his Achille's heel was that although he pretended to despise the others, he really longed to be accepted. He ghosted and covered for them, sometimes going to inordinate lengths, and if he ever became Bolshie they would wheedle him back into a good humour by taking him out to lunch at their clubs. Gladdie and Liza, seething with rage, would send him off with his coat buttoned up correctly and free of dog hairs and with strict instructions that on no account must he agree to write the Chairman's speech for the Chairman's annual address.

'Yes sweetheart, no sweetheart,' Woody would reply.

But of course he always gave in and would come lumbering back very pink in the face, with his tie under one ear and whisper round the door,

'Is the boss about, sweetheart?'

'She's in Sales and Supply.'

'Ah, well listen here, George, I've got a couple of pages to write for the chairman, you'll type them for me like a good girl, won't you? Better not tell the boss…'

Gladdie, who had several sets of eyes in the back of her head, always did find out and Woody and Liza both got lectured. They were a sore trial to her and often had furious fights between themselves but to the rest of the world they presented a united front to the part-time 'butterflies' who went swanning off to garden parties, Ascot, Queen Charlotte's Ball, Wimbledon, the Glorious Twelfth and Twickers, while Woody and his team pounded away on their Banlocks, kept the press sweet, dealt with the outposts in the provinces, and somehow made their department so productive that within two years they had moved on from supplying features to three magazines, to an impressive 280. No matter what a provincial editor wanted they could supply it, from the latest fashions, to a Question and Answer article on the Iron & Steel Bill.

And all the time Woody was teaching Liza the journalist's trade, sometimes throwing her latest article right across the office and shouting,

'You'll never make a bleeding journalist, sweetheart. NEVER!' She would scoop up the pages and retreat in floods of tears and rewrite it all again. It was invaluable training on how to catch the reader's attention: get your facts right; check everything; slant it to the market and keep it to the required length. It was all drummed into her, enabling her to become a full-time freelancer, working for women's magazines, the BBC Radio Four *Today* programme, BBC TV documentaries, writing romantic fiction, children's books and ultimately *The Wombles*.

Woody was such a hard worker himself that he inspired them to keep up with him. He was a born journalist and on the slimmest of briefings he could turn out exactly what was wanted: 750 words on the *Crisis in Management*, *Do we need Stately Homes?* or *Germany Today*, he could provide it. As he was at the same time dealing with an even increasing number of provincial editors – who were in and out of the office all the time – it was a very full life. He dictated like a machine gun and Gladdie and Liza took it in turns to take dictation, reaching a peak on the day when they transcribed and typed eighty-one letters. Liza used to be so tired that she slept all the way back on the Brighton train, dozed in the bus, ate her supper, dozed again and went to bed at 9 pm as she had to get up at 6.30 to catch the 7.20 bus and 8 o'clock train. Gladdie, who lived in Balham with her elderly mother, was equally exhausted, but Woody thrived on it all.

No matter how hard they pounded their ancient Banlocks, the work silted up round them. Woody's desk was Gladdie's despair. The sight of those mounds of letters, articles and files of notes which occasionally avalanched on to the floor, really upset her efficient brain. Between them, Woody and Gladdie persuaded Personnel to engage a new junior which meant that at long last there was somebody actually junior to Liza.

'Now listen, sweetheart,' Woody said one afternoon, his feet up on his overflowing desk, hat on the back of his head, spectacles and tie at half-mast and coat, naturally, buttoned up all wrong. 'Give us a fag. Ta. Now, I'm the marchioness of X, all right?'

Liza tried to imagine the transformation scene. The marchioness had been to the office several times, a very imposing woman with royal connections. Woody proceeded to give her a masterclass on speech writing.

'Right, then George. This is my speech. "When I come home in the evening my husband often says to me"…' and the amazing thing was this gruff, suspicious, kindly, tough, ex-war correspondent could transform himself into a 35-year-old, sophisticated female socialite. If he had been born twenty years later he would have made a fortune as a ghost-writer. When he was just too overworked some of his load was shunted on to Liza and it was invaluable training.

One day, out of the blue, Woody was asked to spend a Friday to Monday with Lord X at his stately home to 'work out' his lordship's forthcoming speech. Gladdie and Liza were almost as pleased and happy as Woody, who dearly loved a peer. They spread the word round the department in an off-hand way. Super Boss and Under Boss and all the butterflies were deeply impressed and the tea-lady gave him a saucer to go with his mug. They brushed his suit – dog hairs in all directions – steamed his tie over the electric kettle, and Gladdie bullied him into going to the barbers in the basement and Ivor, the office boy, who had a photographic memory, wrote him out reams of notes on Lord X and polished his shoes with the washing-up towel. At 5.30 pm on the Friday everyone crowded into the office to wish him luck as he strode off down the marble staircase.

Gladdie and Liza couldn't wait for Monday morning. At last Woody had been recognised for his true worth. They typed away, ears back, listening for his office door. He must have slipped in very quietly because they never heard a thing. At 10.30 Gladdie said uneasily, 'Better have a look…'

He was sitting slumped in front of his desk. Very slowly Woody raised his head. His hair was all over the place, his coat was mis-buttoned and his spectacles were crooked. A very slow tear rolled down one cheek.

'Mr Woodham?'

'Got a cigarette, sweetheart?' There was a long pause and then he said, 'They put me in the Housekeeper's quarters, miss…'

Gladdie didn't say anything to Lord X, but from then on she treated him with glacial politeness and somehow managed things so that Woody was always too busy to do any more ghosting and Lord X found himself shunted firmly in the direction of the Press Officer, who was a nice enough man but, as Ivor said, he should have been a barrister as he was always being called to the bar.

Ivor and Gladdie weren't particularly companionable, but they had a healthy respect for each other. He was a very middle-aged 15, always immaculately dressed in striped trousers and a black coat and five decades before the internet, he was a walking reference book.

'Ivor,' Liza would say frantically as the Banlock clattered jumpily, 'Woody's got John Smith as Chairman of Bedrock and Amalgamated Mines. I'm sure that doesn't sound quite right...'

'Sir John now, Last Honours List. Also OBE, MC, TA Retd, married to the Hon Arabella, daughter of...'

The difficulty was to stop him once he got started, but he was more up to date and far more reliable than the tatty reference books which they, as the least important office, always inherited at the end of the line. Once his fame spread, lures were cast for him to work higher up the scale. But Woody stood firm for once and refused to let him go.

Of course ten minutes later his conscience got the better of him. 'You'd be doing yourself a good turn, George,' he said gloomily. 'Old Super Boss isn't a bad sort really.'

'No thank you, Mr Woodham. I'd rather stay with you,' Ivor said primly. 'You're a good lad.'

Five minutes after that he was yelling, 'Where's that bloody pie-can with my copy?!'

Woody was maddening, unpunctual and verbose. His letters meandered over three pages when four lines was all that was needed. He quite often dictated to Liza as he marched down the echoing marble corridors, raced down the stairs and across the main hall so that she became adept at writing 'George, you miserable old devil you' while on the trot. He had a host of erratic cronies who were forever sliding in and out of his tiny office, trying to borrow money off him or expounding some wildcat scheme for getting rich quick. One of the oddest of them had a kind of brainstorm and locked himself in the Ladies and refused to come out so that they had to send for the carpenter to come and take the door off its hinges. On the other hand, some of his friends were both responsible and eminent so that sometimes, perched on his radiator or the corner of his desk, they would encounter a Royal Academician, George Orwell, Enid Blyton or a brace of Cabinet Ministers.

Liza recalled, 'He continued, although less and less often, to throw my articles or features or ghost speeches across the office and shout, "You'll never make a journalist, you bloody pie-can."' But whatever else there was to complain about, one thing was certain, working for Woody was never dull and it taught Liza a lot.

We were all of us always chronically hard up, but being broke as one of a group isn't nearly as bad as being poor on your own. If you know that your immediate boss, in my case Gladdie, was eating peanut butter sandwiches for five days in a row because she was saving up for her next rail fare, I didn't feel too badly about wearing my old naval greatcoat to parties, and anyway we had all started moonlighting. Gladdie got a job as a waitress three nights a week; Woody, Ivor and I wrote anything for anybody. Ivor, in his late teens by now was particularly good at weighty, rather dull political constituency speeches.

However, Conservative Central Office was also peopled by the well-heeled butterfly set. They were all rather vague and looked upon their jobs as a fill-in period between leaving finishing school and inevitably walking up the aisle of either St Margarets, Westminster, or the Brompton Oratory.

Occasionally Liza crossed the great divide and while wearing her evening dress made of parachute silk, and galloping through the Dashing White Sergeant, would come face to face with one of her colleagues.

'Lizzy, what are you doing here?'

'Having a super time, thank you.'

As Liza's Rifle Brigade escort was definitely about three up on her colleagues, it was a great moment of triumph. It didn't last long. The colleague pulled rank the next week and hauled Liza in to do her filing. There wasn't much of it but she and a couple of other butterflies took the opportunity to do a little social detective work.

'What does your father do?'

'He's dead.'

'Oh ... do you live with your mother then?

'Yes. She runs a boarding house in Brighton.'

'Oh!'

That was a stumper all right and Liza was dismissed back to the office to help Ivor wash up the mugs. They decided to dry them on the window sill and Liza must have been crosser than she realised because one of them went bombing down to smash into smithereens on the pavement four floors below, narrowly missing a hopeful Tory candidate and ending a political career before it started. He looked up, saw their moon-like faces gazing down, shook his fist and marched into the entrance hall. Ivor and Liza took refuge in the library on the fifth floor.

'I dunno, Miss,' said Woody later. 'This place seems to attract nutters. There was this candidate up here saying we were trying to kill 'im. Do you you know anything about it?'

They shook their heads.

'Oh,' said Woody, 'I see ... well another funny thing, we're a mug short...'

The very first person Woody sent Liza to interview *in situ* was the then top author, Angela Thirkell. Liza was a huge fan and had all her books, but the thought of meeting her face to face was extremely daunting and she arrived on her doorstep, with Woody's orders imprinted on her mind, feeling sick with apprehension.

'Ask her about how she manages, get her favourite recipe – don't forget this is a woman's feature article – what clothes does she like, what does she think makes a happy family....'

'What about her feelings for Trollope?'

'We don't want any of that highbrow stuff, Miss. We want the woman's angle. Now scram!'

Liza needn't have worried as when, pale and punctual, she arrived at the Thirkell front door it was opened by a rather irate, youngish man.

'Yes?'

'I-I-I've got an appointment to s-s-see Miss Thirkell.'

'Press?'

'Well yes, that is I suppose so...'

'She never sees the Press.'

The door was shut extremely firmly and Liza slunk back to the office. Woody hunched himself up like a moulting eagle and sighed, aired his views on women in general and Liza, a bloody pie-can who would never make a journalist, and sent her off to interview a Trades' Union charlady who not only asked her in but plied her with cups of tea and her views on everything, including her favourite recipe, which was bread pudding. As she had never been interviewed before and Liza was a complete novice, the result was a horrible mish-mash which sent Woody into a fury.

'Heaven knows what saved me from instant dismissal,' Liza wrote. 'He rewrote the piece which duly appeared under the title *As I Often Say to my Old Man*. It was a small success. There was no by-line but we did have thirty-five letters from charladies living all over the British Isles.'

'We'll make a writer of you yet, Miss,' said Woody, magnanimously forgetting that he'd rewritten the entire piece. 'Now I've got a good idea. You're going to write a ladies column called *Fashion, Food and the Family*. What do you think of that, George?'

Although Liza couldn't cook, was still wearing her service castoffs, and was unmarried with absolutely no experience of motherhood, it still seemed that she was the ideal candidate for the job. Chauvinism may have had nothing to do with it, but it is a curious fact that if you were a recognisably female journalist/writer your boss/editor would take it as a matter of course that you knew instinctively.

I went to my first fashion show. The great thing was to look as old as possible. Teenagers wore flowering hats, white gloves, 'pearls', dressy dresses, high heels and carried large bulky, square-shaped 'cases' and elegant umbrellas. All this added years to your appearance and we all firmly believed that we looked about 35. Needless to say, most of my outfit was borrowed so I arrived wearing a friend's suit, Ma's elderly fox fur, one of the butterfly's many hats, a very cheap model's case and carrying Gladdie's umbrella. It wasn't easy edging past the other journalists and on to a little gilt chair. There was a fairly frosty welcome for the new girl.

We were a very mixed bunch. The girls in the front three rows all wore tremendous hats, fur stoles, enormously square shouldered suits and high heels with ankle straps no matter how like tree stumps their legs were. Gloves, pearls and disdainful expressions were the order of the day. They also had jangling bracelets, brollies with frills and enormous square-shaped hand bags. If the skirts had been two feet longer we wouldn't have been out of place at an Edwardian tea party.

Behind the front rows the standard of clothes deteriorated demonstrating a sharp divide between fashion writers and mere reporters. Both sides despised each other and as Liza never fitted into either camp they both ignored her.

However, we all used the same awful language to describe the clothes. Skirts were 'pencil' or 'arrow' slim, whatever that really meant, until the New Look overwhelmed us when shirts became 'swirling', vests were eye-catching, accessories were 'touches of white at the neck and cuffs'. Petticoats 'frothed', nylons were 'sheer' and there were 'Highwayman' coats for those who are one up on the 'swing back'.

All the fashion PROs were immensely formidable, so was the top model of day, Barbara Goalen, who used to throw herself at us with a look of utter scorn. She got me in her sights and I was like a hypnotised rabbit. Interviewing Hardy Amies was even more scaring. He had a PA with him and addressed me through him and looked over my head. Norman Hartnell was much more relaxed, but a bit vague as to who I was or why I was there.

Interviewing the experts for the 'Food' section was quite different. They were plump, jolly, bossy and often alarmingly hearty.

A great many of them appeared to have been at school together and as food rationing still had us in its grip they had to be very inventive.

'Old Joan's macaroons were never very good in Dom Sci in the sixth form,' said Hilda, giving me a hefty buffet on the shoulders as she banged down a plate in front of me in the model kitchen of their firm's PR department, 'but they're splendid now!'

'Just wait until you tase Hildy's tomato and swede pie,' Joan replied with a look which would have curdled the top of the milk. 'Then you'll know what secret weapon we really used on those Jerry subs!'

Something about which Liza did know a bit, but was silenced by the Official Secrets Act.

Divided they might be on their various specialities, but they were endlessly inventive. 'Of course we couldn't have cooked any of this without pro-fat margarine. Have another helping, Lizzie.'

Liza ate her way stolidly through everything, being extremely hungry, and when Trissie somehow acquired two lemons, she held an auction in the dining room and raised quite a lot of money for the Red Cross.

All free samples from the PR kitchens were devoured without comment by Gladdie and Ivor. Liza cribbed and rewrote the 'family' bits from women's magazines. The provincial editors, all male, latched on to the column as a good way of collecting female readers and at one heady moment it was syndicated in over 300 magazines and newspapers. It brought kudos to Woody and an extra £1/10s a week to Liza, so everybody was happy – and Woody decided to launch Liza as a film critic:

As I'd always been a great movie buff, it was a surprisingly easy thing to do. All that was needed was to ring up the major film companies and ask to be put on their viewing list. It was marvellous to leave the office at ten to slide into the Odeon, Leicester Square to see Gregory Peck or James Stewart. Occasionally the stars themselves would be there and hold court with senior members of the press.

On a few heady occasions I sat next to the highly respected critic Milton Schulman, who had a torch attached to his pen so that we could see what we were both writing on our programmes. The great trick about writing film reviews was to get the title and the name of the stars in the first two lines after which it didn't seem to matter much what you wrote as long as it was complimentary. Just once I wrote what I really thought and the film company, who seemed to have spies everywhere, wrote to Super Boss complaining about me.

'Don't try to be clever, George,' said Woody.

Liza, earning an extra one pound five shillings a week from this particular feature, swallowed any embryonic ideas of artistic integrity and complied. The reward was a third column on Radio and TV. Radio came first in those days and, in addition to getting all the regulation handouts, it meant actually interviewing some of the stars. One way and another she was now earning eight pounds a week and some noble soul in accounts felt it only right to send a confidential memo to Super Boss pointing out this was the same salary as his secretary received. The CCO hierarchy was horrified. Memos flew back and forth and Personnel was called in to settle things.

'Mr Woodham, this is an impossible situation and Miss Beresford cannot be allowed to earn the same as Miss S who is a senior secretary of may years standing. Beresford is only a shorthand typist!' (And a pretty inferior one at that was clearly implied.)

'I quite understand, Miss. now why don't I take you out to lunch and we can talk it over...'

Gladdie and Ivor rallied round, forming an instant trade union, each of them loyally swearing that if Liza went, they went. Ivor was all for getting up a petition and a very refined woman from down the corridor came to pay her condolences. Apparently she loved any office disaster and hated married life as she despised her lorry-driver husband whom she always referred to as 'being in transport'. She hadn't got a good word to say for her daughter and son-in-law who lived with her in a very small house which they shared with six dogs. The dogs she adored. She once told Liza that she had tried to commit suicide by putting her head in the oven.

'Oh Mrs Jay, how awful. What happened?'

'Unfortunately it was an electric oven.'

Nothing was ever on her side. She bustled in to the office, her face glowing with the anticipation of disaster.

'If aye were you, Lizzie, aye wouldn't stand for it. Disgraceful aye call it.'

'She isn't standing for it,' said Gladdie, who despised poor Mrs Jay. The feeling was mutual and Mrs Jay ignored Gladdie's remark and went on.

'Aye wouldn't treat one of may little doggies like this.'

'I think I'll write to *The Times*' said Ivor. 'It's victimisation, Lizzy. You must take a stand on behalf of office workers everywhere. The whole of the ideal of private enterprise is at stake!'

It was obvious that Liza was about to be responsible for the first walk-out strike ever at Conservative Central Office so she began clearing out her desk and rehearsing the words with which she would tell Trissie that she had got the sack. Jobs were still too few and far between for anybody to ever dream of expecting their friends to sacrifice themselves on a matter of principle.

Woody returned in the middle of the afternoon. Liza had her speech ready for him.

'Mr Woodham,' I said shakily, 'I just want to say how much I've enjoyed working for you and thank you for teaching me so much. But I would like to hand in my notice because...'

'What the hell are you gassing on about, George?'

'Getting the sack.'

'Oh that! Well of course we can't have you earning the same as a senior secretary.'

'So I'll leave at the end of the week.'

'You'll do what you are told, George. Personnel and I agree you'll never make a seketary.'

'No, Mr Woodham, so...'

'Shut up you bloody pie-can, so we've decided to make you a Press Assistant. When you're not being more thick-headed than usual you can at least write a feature. One day you might even become a real journalist. Now 'op it and get your notebook, I've got a lot of dictation for you.'

'Oh th-thank you, Mr Woodham, I'm really...'

"OP IT!'

Throughout the late 1940s, Liza became engaged and disengaged and re-engaged, quite often to the same person. Trissie had started saying, 'Let me see, how old are you, Elisabeth? Twenty-one and still not married...' and rapidly getting past it, her tone implied. Liza was still young enough to work hard and play hard and went to dances, quite often going to sleep on her partner's shoulders, or with her head on the dinner table.

She was easily drawn to a handsome face and didn't have Portia's discernment about what lay beneath the surface. She was attractive and vivacious and a tremendous flirt, but she missed the biggest coup of the year when she was asked to make up a foursome at the annual HAC Ball. Her blind date was very nice but he had two big drawbacks: he was going bald and he was getting on a bit – 30 at least. It was a spectacular party in the City with a funfair attached to it on a bomb site. The girls looked lovely as they whirled past on the merry-go-round with their long parachute silk dresses billowing. A ride cost 2½d and her 'middle-aged' partner paid for three rides which she enjoyed enormously, but her conscience got the better of her when he asked if she would like a fourth.

'Are you sure you can afford it?' she asked anxiously.

He looked a bit startled but reckoned that he probably could so off she floated again.

He took me home in a taxi, all the way back to the Pont Street flat where six of us were sleeping on the floor. He asked me out to lunch the following week but although he behaved like an uncle, I took fright and mumbled an excuse and fled for dear life. Very old men I could handle, but middle-aged men who spent money like water were outside my range of experience. Anyway I felt guilty about how much I had already cost him. It was about a fortnight later that I discovered that he was a millionaire.

One evening while she was dozing comfortably on her escort's shoulder in a nice quiet, dimly lit nightclub, she became aware that a royal VIP had quite definitely got her eye on him.

He hauled me round as a bulwark and we slid backwards onto the dance floor. The VIP was not in the least deterred, she merely dispatched her equerry to our table with an invitation. It was a very nice invitation, too; she wanted him to take her home.

'Her palace or mine?' said my escort in a frenzy of terror.

The equerry sized up the situation and dealt with it with tact, diplomacy and delicacy. Which means that we left the nightclub about four minutes later like two terrified rabbits. We took our custom to another club where Johnny Weismuller asked me if I'd like to 'bong bongo, bongo' down in the jungle with him. I was all for saying, 'You Tarzan, me Lizzy', but was frightened out of it by his ferocious girlfriend suddenly appearing.

She never dared to tell Trissie about the nightclubs because to her they were on a footing with pubs, although with a rather better class of patron lying about dead drunk.

One night I ran it rather close as *The Tatler* photographer suddenly appeared out of the pulsating gloom and as his camera flashed I slid under the table. It made an interesting picture when it appeared, as in the centre of it were two extremely startled young men, one apparently gazing at his socks.

Trissie was always asking who these people were who kept inviting Liza to their parents when she rarely brought any of them back to meet her. As meeting Trissie for the first time was roughly equivalent to being on the other side of a desk with a light directed full in your eyes, only the bravest and the most determined made their way down into the Brighton basement.

Trissie would begin to relax her façade when she realised that the young men were not the hunting, lascivious wolves of her imagination, but relatively harmless, soon-to-be-out-of-work members of HM Forces. If the two local night staff didn't, or couldn't, turn up for their shift at the boarding house, it was not unusual to find a Rifle Brigade Major and an RNVR Lieut-Commander wearing aprons and helping out. Liza modestly swore that it wasn't for love of her, but rather for the cooking which in some mysterious and marvellous way was still kept up to an amazingly high standard.

Miss Ford, the lodger, loved it all. The military men acquired gin and cigarettes for her and she managed somehow to transform her top floor front into a smoky 1920s night club. Miss Butler bowed graciously, the Misses Thirkell nodded and smiled and nobody minded if the men had two helpings of everything.

It was as Liza approached her 22nd birthday that Trissie started to change her tactics from, 'Yes, he's very nice, but he wants to go and live in Australia', to, 'I see that Jane is getting married. Now let me see, wasn't she in the same form as you at school?' For Trissie, being married wasn't the beginning of something, it was the triumphant finale – despite her own disappointment in that quarter. 'A bad marriage is better than no marriage,' was dropped in to the conversation more and more often. Trissie's wish to see her married off was soon to be granted.

Liza first met the broadcaster Max Robertson in 1947 at a Conservative Party Conference at the Brighton Dome. He was working for the BBC European Service with his eyes firmly fixed on crossing the great divide from the Bush House to Broadcasting House and joining what was then the Home Service, but he had no interest in politics. He said the evening was memorable for two things: being in the same room as Winston Churchill and meeting Liza. At the cocktail party for the press, Woody, cast a jaundiced eye over the seething mass and said to Liza, 'Go and cheer up that miserable looking devil over there, sweetheart.' So she did. In his autobiography *Stop Talking and Give the Score*, Max, who loathed dancing, remembered that his 'contemplation was interrupted by a charming, bubbling and very pretty girl with a sweet smile, that really did curl up the corners of her mouth in a cupid's bow, who came up and asked me to dance. I was completely taken aback and went quietly!'

They were both engaged to other people at the time so no romance flourished at this point. It was not until 1949 that they met again, when they saw each other socially on quite a number of occasions. Max was a very forceful personality who had met Liza's brothers Tristram and Marcus at Cambridge. The least clubbable of men, he did not feel that Cambridge was his milieu and left after the first term to take part in a gold-prospecting expedition to Papua New Guinea. When that proved fruitless he travelled on to Australia and got a job with the Australian Broadcasting Commission. It was the first rung on his very successful radio and television career. At the tender age of 22 he married an Australian girl, Nancy Suttor, who was three years older, and they had two sons, Anthony and Martin. He brought them all back to England at the outbreak of war when he joined the British Army. The marriage, perhaps entered into when they were too young, did not last and a divorce followed in 1947. Now aged 33, Max was a very attractive and forceful man, there were plenty of other women in his life, but it was at a moment when they were both unattached that he asked Liza to go and stay with him and some Dutch friends, the van Swols, who lived in Amsterdam. Hans van Swols was in the Dutch tennis team and he and his English wife, Valerie, proved to be delightful hosts and Liza was entranced by them, their luxurious apartment in Amsterdam, and the fun of being away from austerity Britain in a country full of well-dressed, well-fed, kindly people. She wrote:

It was unbelievable to go to a fashion show to see somewhat portly models wearing beautiful, unrationed clothes. The price tags were about the equivalent of ten weeks of my salary so buying anything was out of the question. However, you could buy as much chocolate as you liked. A little went a long way with me and I watched round-eyed as the women munched their way through a four-course meal and then half a box of really rich chocolates.

Max chose his moment well and asked Liza to marry him. She recalled:

I said yes because I liked him and got on really well with his parents, and anyway we were living in a total fairyland. In five days I'd be back at my Banlock and rations and all this would have vanished. Which only goes to show that you should never underestimate the determination of the Scots and the BBC.

In *Stop Talking and Give the Score*, Max related the circumstances of their engagement in a business-like way:

While in Amsterdam, I managed to persuade Liza to become engaged and even to agree to a quick wedding. She probably said 'yes', thinking there was no way I could bring it about. Fortunately for me, I had to come back in the middle of that week to co-host *Picture Page* with Joan Gilbert, since her regular colleague, Leslie Mitchell, was unavailable. It was a great chance for me, for it was my first appearance in any important TV studio programme.

To the amusement of those I was working with, I spent all my spare time on the telephone, arranging a registrar's marriage in Brighton followed by a Blessing Ceremony at St Colomba's Church near Harrods. Having completed these swift arrangements, I returned to Amsterdam triumphant.

Liza's side of the story was that,

He was gone for 24 hours, during which time I was taken round the canals and to the Rembrandt exhibition and my Dutch friends' boxer dog ate my passport except for one corner. Explaining this to the police took quite a lot of time and Max was back almost before I knew he'd gone. Hans and I went to pick him up at Schiphol airport. He looked very pleased with himself.

'Well,' he said, 'It's all arranged.'

'What is?'

'Our wedding. We fly back on Monday and we get married on Tuesday. I've got a special licence and a wedding ring. I've booked the Registry Office in Brighton. Doctor Hemming and Aden will be witnesses and Aden will give you away. He'll take you there in his car, then there'll be a blessing ceremony at St Colomba's Church, Pont St, with my parents and friends. And Lady Blane is giving the reception at her home in Chelsea.'

I literally could not speak. He took my hand and patted it.

'It's all right,' he said. 'I've told your Mother!'

The press made much of it with the headline 'Eight Day Courtship', which of course it had not been, and Max spent the first day of their honeymoon interviewing the ladies of the Burwash Women's Institute, doubtless with a bemused Liza in tow.

Chapter 4

The Frantic Fifties

Liza and Max began their married life in his bedsit in Nepean Street, Roehampton, south-west London. Max made it quite clear from the start that there was no way Liza could give up working nor, one suspects, would she have ever wished to do so as she was finding the urge to write increasingly compulsive. She continued to work for Woody at Central Office which was in the throes of preparing for a general election in February 1950. Max wrote to his Aunt Eddie, 'We are continuing to live in my old digs until after the election. As you may imagine, Liza's department at the CCO is very busy now and will get busier as the election fright grows stronger.'

Three weeks before the election Liza wrote to her mother-in-law:

> We are working very much in fits and starts – some nights I don't get away until seven but some of the girls are working until 10 so I don't feel I have much to complain of. The staff are all very hopeful about the result and I must say it is very cheering the way requests are pouring in from newspapers all over the country asking for articles on Conservative policy and the Tory point of view.

In fact, the Labour Government was returned to power but with a much reduced majority of five.

Meanwhile, Max was becoming an established member of the BBC Staff, based at Bush House in the Strand but increasingly involved in BBC television, which was then in its infancy. He was working on a wide variety of programmes, mainly outside broadcasts (OBs), alongside the likes of Wynford Vaughan-Thomas, John Snagge, Stuart MacPherson and Brian Johnston.

In 1950, Liza became pregnant, somewhat to Max's displeasure; already having two sons from his first marriage, he was not in favour of more children. It was obvious that their 'digs' no longer met their accommodation requirements, and Max heard of a flat that had just come on the market, 25 Cyril Mansions, opposite Battersea Park, one of several mansion blocks in Prince of Wales Drive. It was a large, roomy flat but had one drawback: it was on the top floor and there was no lift. There were ninety-six stairs to the top floor, which they shared with the Jacquellos, a young actor and his wife. Their rent was £5 a week.

Of her pregnancy, Liza recalled:

I just got larger and larger and had to stay home. Mother gave me two maternity smocks and an expandable skirt (second-hand clothes were still in short supply) and as there were no books on babies and starting a family I had to do my best by asking for advice. Fortunately, Max's wonderful mother came to stay with us just before the baby was due. She made Max some proper meals so that he could stop feeding at the BBC canteen [Liza's culinary skills were practically non-existent], and she tried to teach me some baby care. The wartime shortages were to go on for some time and shampoo, soap and any clothes were all donated by kind friends.

The day finally dawned, January 31st 1951, when the baby decided to make her entrance. Max went over to the Jaquellos to use their phone to call an ambulance. When we heard it arrive at the end of Prince of Wales Drive we started the slow journey down the ninety-six stairs. The ambulance had stopped and the back door was open and two men were waiting for us; suddenly it all got too much for Max who turned pale green. The men rushed to help him and I was abandoned while they fussed over him. I had awful visions of the baby being born on the pavement when luckily they remembered me. It wasn't born in the ambulance but it was a close run thing and I was whisked into Queen Charlotte's Hospital just in time to give birth to Kate. Mother R came to the rescue again and moved in to help with the baby.

Max's parents, Alan and Renée Robertson, whom Liza adored, had retired and come home before the war from India where Alan, an engineer, had run the Dacca, and subsequently the Calcutta, Railway system. 'Father R' as he was known within the family, was a short, white-haired and moustached, twinkly-eyed realist. In the nineteenth century, his grandfather had

Liza aged about 18 months with her father, novelist 'JD' Beresford aged 58.

Beatrice Evelyn Roskams (Trissie) c.1900.

The Beresford children c.1930. (Left to right) Tristram, Liza, Aden, Marcus.

Trissie, Liza and Annie Rhodes, Liza's nanny, in Torquay 1934.

Liza Beresford WRNS.

Liza in Victoria Street, London, 1948, on her way to Conservative Central Office.

Liza at about the time she met Max Robertson.

At Max's parents' house, Gibbet Oak. (Left to right, back row) Bob Carswell (brother-in-law), Liza, Renée Robertson holding granddaughter Kate, Marian Carswell (Max's sister), the Carswell Nanny, Alan Robertson. (Front row) Judy the Sealyham, Penny and Gill Carswell. Bob Carswell ran a tea plantation in Ceylon and the family had come back for a holiday.

Max and Liza with baby Marcus and Kate in the garden at Number 4 after Marcus's christening 1956.

Liza and Max were off to Lambeth Palace for the wedding of his secretary Diana to Humphrey Fisher, son of the Archbishop of Canterbury.

Marcus, Liza, Kate, Max and Miss Tibbs the cat in the sitting room at Number 4 in 1957. Liza's first book *The Television Mystery* had just been published.

Liza on continuity in Grenada 1957.

Max and Liza opened St Anne's church bazaar more than once in the 1950s. The vicar was Fr Shells who when made Canon Shells, modestly said that his promotion was inevitable given his name.

Vox pop. A staged interview with a taxi driver – there is no sign of a recorder.

Liza's first view of 22 Little St, Alderney in 1964. By 1978 it had doubled in size.

Liza and Max with Gladdie and Trissie.　　　　Max, Marcus and Kate 1964.

No 4 Earlsfield Rd in the 1960s. Liza can just be seen about to get her Minivan out of the garage.

Liza in the Central Office of Information studio with Ivor Mills.

Liza on the rocks in Alderney. This was probably taken as a guide to the artwork for her Alderney musical, *The Little Mermaid*.

The garden at Spencer Park. The magical 'secret' park is behind the wall at the bottom of the garden.

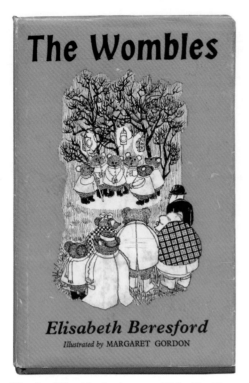

The first Wombles book was published by Ernest Benn in 1968. The most recent reissue was in 2010, published by Bloomsbury in paperback.

Liza discusses a Wombles script with animator Ivor Wood at the FilmFair studio.

Ivor adjusts Tobermory with Orinoco and Wellington looking on. (*Supplied by Tom Sanders*)

Ivor Wood in the recording studio with Bernard Cribbins, the 'voice of the Wombles'. (*Supplied by Tom Sanders*)

Wellington, Great Uncle Bulgaria and Orinoco ready for action. (*Alamy*)

Liza is greeted by Great Uncle Bulgaria as she opens the Womble burrow at Cannizzaro Park 1974.

Liza in the garden at No 3 Spencer Park.

Liza and Great Uncle Bulgaria departing for South Africa on board RMS *Windsor Castle*. Note the appropriate sign! (*Alamy*)

It's party time at No 22. Liza's canapés were about to be shut away in her office, hidden from Archie the cat who always enjoyed a good party, especially the food.

Max and Liza at the Sinbad Hotel, Malindi, Kenya in 1982.

Station Master duties at Braye Station.

1989. The scriptwriter steals a scene as an extra in
Rosebud and the Murder on the Alderney Express.

A nod is as good as a wink for Judge Sir
Arlott Johns (John Arlott) at Rosebud's trial.

Journalist John Passmore, former Womble columnist, catching up with Liza after he returned from
Tiananmen Square, Beijing, from where he reported on the massacre for the *London Evening Standard*.

Liza on the set of the half-hour specials. She is holding her offspring – Bungo (Kate) and Orinoco (Marcus). Outside the burrow are Tomsk, Great Uncle Bulgaria, Wellington and new character Cairngorm MacWomble the Terrible (Max).

Charlie, 4, and Ben, 2, watch *The Wombles* on television with Granny Liza in her study.

Liza with her trusty colonel outside No 22. Note the rust!

Liza's long-standing Alderney friends, Jenny Gosney and Maggie Burridge, 'exchange news' in the kitchen while Liza recycles a birthday card.

Marcus, Liza and Kate at Buckingham Palace after Liza received her MBE. Great Uncle Bulgaria watches approvingly from the window sill.

Liza with Alderney Womble and Orinoco on Wimbledon Common in 1998 at the press launch of the new Cinar Womble animations.

Marianne, Charlie, Ben and Marcus with Marcus's alter ego Orinoco, on Wimbledon Common.

Liza with Orinoco and Great Uncle Bulgaria in 1998 photographed for a spread in *OK! Magazine*. (*Copyright Alan Strutt*)

Liza gets her hands dirty in the greenhouse. Gardening was her relaxation and she loved growing her own vegetables.

Liza at her usual seat in the kitchen with Polly, Archie's successor.

Liza at Alderney Airport in 2000 with her family, Kate, Charlie, Marianne, Ben and Marcus.

moved down from Aberdeen to Patrixbourne in Kent, where he began his career in Holy Orders as a curate. He ended it as the Canon Librarian at Canterbury Cathedral and on his death he left his family in sound economic standing. His son, Alan's father, decided to leave a job in the City and live the life of a gentleman of leisure. All too soon, the money began to run out and Alan was taken out of Cheltenham College and apprenticed to an engineering firm in Kent. His sole ambition had been to be a farmer, instead he found himself in India running railways. In the war, at the age of 57, he volunteered and was accepted as an Adjutant in the RAF, and then after a few false starts, he achieved his dream when he and Renée bought Gibbet Oak Farm, not far from Tenterden, Kent, where 'Father R' grew apples commercially.

He was at his happiest walking through the orchards in his three-piece country tweed, gumboots and brown derby, puffing on his pipe. He was the prototype for Great Uncle Bulgaria, patriarch of the Wombles.

Gibbet Oak was a fascinating old house. The original, half-timbered section was pre-Tudor, with later Georgian and Victorian brick-built extensions on either side. There was a passage from the kitchen at the back of the house to the front door and every morning, when the back door was opened, Mary the duck would waddle through with her gang of ducklings from the garden, along the ancient wooden passage and out of the front door to the pond. The original Gibbet – an ancient and almost hollow oak tree, stood sentinel by the drive; it was said to have been used as a gibbet to hang smugglers, before Romney Marsh was drained and Tenterden became a 'limb' of the Cinque Ports. Behind the main house was an Oast, various ancient outbuildings, a walled kitchen garden, the farm manager's house, tractor and apple packing sheds and then orchards and woodland. The house provided a country idyll, an escape from the pressures of London for Liza and, subsequently, her children. It was to Gibbet Oak that Liza briefly repaired while she got used to being a mother, under the auspices of 'Mother R'.

Back in London, it soon became apparent that getting a baby and a pram up ninety-six steps was not practical. Work was going well for Max and Liza was busy working as a freelance contributor to CCO from home. It was time to buy a family house. Coincidentally, Trissie, now 70, thought it was time to retire from running the house in Kemp Town and she and Max, both forceful characters who rarely saw eye to eye, agreed a truce, and it was decided that she would move up to London and live with the Robertsons and help with the cooking.

A surveyor friend of Max's turned up trumps – he had heard of a large Victorian villa which was coming onto the market. Built in 1883 and situated at the top of Earlsfield Road, on the edge of Wandsworth Common, it was semi-detached, had three floors and six bedrooms. There was a front garden, a back garden, the remains of a bombed conservatory, and a garage. The purchase price was £2,000. Wandsworth in the early 1950s was a very unfashionable place to live and the exodus from Chelsea was just a trickle as prices began to rise north of the river. It was at least another twenty years before black cabs would agree to cross the river without a great deal of grumbling or a downright refusal.

Trissie travelled up from the coast to inspect the premises and gave it her imprimatur, deciding immediately which room she wanted. It was at the back of the house on the first floor and down two stairs so that it was slightly separated from the rest of the family. It had three windows from which she could keep an eye on people and a washroom.

Trissie's hand was at the kitchen tiller once more and the war of the wills – her's and Max's – began, and was to continue for nearly twenty years with Liza locked in the middle. Madame Cholet had entered her kitchen kingdom.

Max was away working when the move took place in November 1951. He was covering the Royal Tour of Canada with John Snagge and as he travelled from location to location across the length and breadth of Canada, he sent Liza almost daily letters instructing her on the dos and don'ts of the purchase. As Max was playing deck tennis with Snagge, the Duke of Edinburgh and the Duke's equerry, Lt Cdr Michael Parker, on board the *Empress of Scotland*, steaming her way back across the Atlantic, Liza was grappling with the logistics of house purchase. Somehow it all happened more or less according to plan, and she, the baby, plus Trissie moved in to 4 Earlsfield Road; Max joined them later, on his triumphant return.

The neighbours in the attached house were a Scottish family, Doctor Mitchell, his wife Mona and adult daughter, Margaret. He was a very kind man and always willing to come round at moment's notice to treat any ailment and put the world to right with a glass of sherry, or better still whisky. On the other, detached, side lived the Pullen family. The patriarch was old Mr Pullen, a tough character with dubious connections to the underworld. His wife came from a gypsy family and she was small, dark and gentle; one of their sons, Charlie, was in his teens. Thin, with dark, curly hair, he used to ride his horse bareback up Earlsfield Road, ride it straight through their house and into their back garden, where he would tether and feed it.

When old Mr Pullen died, Liza was accorded the great honour of being invited to pay her respects and was taken to see the body, which was lying in state in the 'front room'.

He looked very peaceful and was surrounded by flowers. His was the second dead body I had seen and again you could see that the person no longer existed and this was nothing but an empty shell. It was very comforting. A most imposing line of big black Daimlers bearing other members of the family and friends drove slowly up the road with more mourners walking along the side. Mr Pullen's closed casket was carried out by his big muscular sons and placed in the hearse which had DAD picked out in flowers. There was quite a police presence on duty, too. Slowly the procession moved on and it wasn't until later that we were told that old Pullen was an important member of the South West Gang. There was a lot of gang warfare in London in those days and we realised that we were 'safe' because we lived next door to the Pullens. The family moved out and sometime later one of the daughters got in touch with me and said would I write to her mother as she wasn't well and missed us all. I did my best to be entertaining, describing Mrs Sewards opposite who had opened a nursery school. It was very useful for Katy who loved it. Luckily Mother never found out but Mrs Pullen loved hearing about her old neighbourhood and when she died all my letters were found spread round her on the bed. She was buried with them.

The grim, dark silhouette of Wandsworth Prison, the other side of the railway line from Earlsfield Road, was a constant reminder of what could happen to lawbreakers. Mrs Wootton, the Robertson's first 'Daily' at No 4, was married to a prison warder and would cheerfully turn up to work with the news that someone had 'taken the long drop' early that morning. When the Great Train Robber Ronnie Biggs escaped from the prison in the 1960s, the siren's baleful wail put the wind up Trissie, who insisted on searching under every bed in No 4 for the escaped prisoner.

To make the living in the large house viable, the Robertsons took in lodgers on the top floor with its three sizeable bedrooms. They acquired a somewhat silent young man called Terence from the Foreign Office. He did open up a bit as he got to know the family better and years later Liza read a bit about him in the newspapers. He was by then a First Secretary posted to a British Embassy in Eastern Europe. When the Russians rolled through the country's capital in their tanks, Terence very bravely went to meet them on the steps of the embassy where he told them firmly and politely it was politically private property. Eventually they rumbled off. Subsequently, he told Liza that throughout the confrontation he had to keep his hand in his trouser pockets because they were trembling so much.

Another lodger, Robin Hancox, was only 18 when he arrived and training as a law student. He became a life-long friend of Liza's.

I saw him off on his first case which earned him 18/6d. We were so proud of him and it was the start of a great career which led to him becoming the Chief Justice in Kenya and earned him an OBE. I went with him and his mother, Lady Wicks, to Buckingham Palace.

London, even inner suburbs like Wandsworth, was still feeling the after effects of the war. Confectionery and sugar rationing ended in 1953 and meat in 1954. There was still plenty of evidence of wartime bombing raids, where streets looked like rows of rotten teeth where only a black stump of a bombed house remained. Make-do-and-mend was very much the tenet by which most people lived and none more so than Liza. She was already a Womble before her time.

Another drawback of London life was smog, or 'pea-soupers' as they were known. Most households burned coal fires in the winter producing vast quantities of smoke which would get trapped in the atmosphere at ground level. Buildings were black with soot and so were Londoners' lungs. The Great Smog of 1952 was the worst such incident Liza remembered.

There was a street lamp lighter who came round every evening on his bicycle and lit the tall lamp outside the Mitchells', using a long pole. But sometimes this made no difference at all as the dreaded smog slowly grew thicker and drowned everything. Both men and women wore a sort of home-made yashmak and London's suburbs would come to a halt. It was my duty to write to Mother R every Sunday. If she didn't get my letter by Tuesday I was in trouble. On one particular day the smog was really thick by the afternoon. With my letter in my overcoat pocket and my yashmak in place, I opened the front door. You could see about a foot in front of you. With my hands outstretched I located the garden gate. By bending down I could just about see the road kerb. There was only one thing for it – I got down on my hands and knees and located the gutter and then the kerb. It was deathly quiet – as if you'd suddenly gone deaf. I crawled across the street to the opposite kerb. There were no other pedestrians, no cars, no aircraft. London had come to a complete standstill. It seemed a long crawl to the post box and then there was the return journey. By the time I got back, Mother was standing by the front door, calling my name in the foul, dirty air and even her voice was muffled!

The smog lasted several days and it coated everything in the house: clothing, mirrors, chair covers. It hung in a yellow blur round the lights. The only good point was that it put you out like an anaesthetic at night. God help anyone who had breathing problems. When the Clean Air Act came in it was literally a life saver. Coal fires and smoking factory chimneys vanished forever.

Liza was beginning to get work via Max's BBC contacts as well as continuing to write pieces for Woody at Conservative Central Office. In 1952 she tested unsuccessfully as a television announcer and confided in Renée that she was 'trying to write a novelette in my spare moments. There is supposed to be a big market for them and it is a nice, simple story to write … so far.' That didn't come to anything but the following year she wrote that 'I am now doing a new series of articles on Famous Women for the Conservatives which means a (tiny) bit more money. I am also cooperating with a woman who used to be a scriptwriter on a television play. Hope it works.' Liza also began her long association with BBC Radio (then the Light Programme) working on an ad hoc basis for *Woman's Hour* as a very lowly reporter, and once a fortnight for an overseas programme,

Calling Newfoundland. The programme was housed in a hotel diametrically opposite Broadcasting House at the bottom of Portland Place. It called for a lot of ingenuity to find a topic which was remotely connected with that faraway country but she needed the five guineas so that was that.

In 1953 Max decided to go freelance and the first job offered to him was to be the chairman of *Panorama*, which had just been launched unsuccessfully, and BBC TV was looking for a replacement anchorman. *Panorama* was a very different beast in those days, more of a magazine programme than one of investigative journalism or political debate. Max was an able linkman, quick on his feet and able to respond to any problems – the programme was live – but he was not, as he admitted, the right man for in-depth discussion or debate. Malcolm Muggeridge, then Editor of *Punch* magazine, was brought in to provide the sharper edge to interviews. Liza was somewhat sceptical about the programme. In letters to her mother-in-law she observed:

Tuesday, 16 February 1954 Max was rehearsing all day at Lime Grove for *Panorama*, I doubt if that programme is going to last.

Friday 26 March 1954 Went with Max to Lime Grove. I interviewed David Attenborough. He was very kind and produced a flood of information about his programmes and I just scribbled away in my notebook.

July 13th 1954 Uncertainty about Max's *Panorama* future. Malcolm Muggeridge is in the game for it. I am in Sheffield at the moment on a job but only for a couple of hours and now in the train returning to London. I have had two articles published in *Woman* which is encouraging and I'm busy collecting material for more.

By 1955 Liza was pregnant once again. 'I am to have a baby in the autumn or late summer,' she told Renée, but sadly she miscarried early on. 'Went to the TV Awards at the Scott Theatre and then on to the dance at Grosvenor House. Home to find signs of miscarriage,' she recorded baldly.

One of the great advantages of working for radio was that the BBC trained reporters in how to use recording equipment, and as they were not allowed to take a recorder on public transport, the BBC paid for taxis.

Based in Wandsworth, this was not always easy and the obvious solution was for Liza to have her own car. Max somehow managed to find £400 and bought Liza a Morris Minor. It was a practical car which could be parked in the front drive – but there was a drawback: Liza couldn't drive. Luckily there was a driving school at the bottom of Earlsfield Rd, run by a very kind and tolerant man, Mr Donavan.

He not only had the patience of a saint but also the courage of a hero. He needed it. I was hopeless. Luckily there was hardly any other traffic about and at last he taught me where the brake was. I did hit the back of another car once but wonderful Mr Donovan somehow sorted out the situation and as I hadn't done any damage to the other car the driver eventually drove off muttering.

The lessons reached the thirty mark before I took the test yet again and by this time I was pregnant and I felt lousy. Everybody turned out to watch me drive jerkily away. None of us thought I had a hope in hell of passing. Fortunately the local streets were very quiet. I managed to give exaggerated hand signals as Mr Donovan had drilled into me, stopped at the yellow traffic lights and luckily didn't get around to reversing before I just had to stop. I drew to a halt, switched off and put my head on the steering wheel feeling terrible as everything swum round me.

'Don't you feel well?' The examiner asked.

'Going to have a baby … oooh…'

'What now?!'

I mutely shook my head and we sat in silence while I tried to fight the sickness. The examiner gripped his test papers and said in a very fast voice.

'What do the red lights mean?'

'Stop'

'How do you signal you're turning right?'

'Put out your right hand.'

'What does the green light mean?'

'Go ahead.'

'You've passed,' he gabbled. 'Can you get us back?'

It was only a matter of yards and he couldn't wait to get out of the car. He handed the papers over to the astounded Mr Donovan and drove off. I don't think it was anything to do with me, but Mr Donovan and his young family emigrated to Australia and he named his youngest child Elizabeth after me and I have often wondered what happened to Elizabeth Donovan. I hope she was a better driver than I was.

The baby was due in early February 1956. Max was sent by the BBC to cover the Winter Olympics which were held in Cortina where he worked both for radio and television, leaving Liza in the care of Trissie and a specialist, Miss Bishop. On 4 February, Liza was admitted to a private nursing home in Balham – just in time as she produced a son, Marcus Craigie, almost immediately. Somehow the BBC got hold of the news. Max was waiting for the cue to start transmission to commentate on the ice hockey match between Russia and the USA when the announcer in London cued over to him with the words '…and now we join our commentator in Cortina, Max Robertson. By the way, Max, it's a boy, congratulations.' Max managed to stammer out something along the lines of 'thank you very much, but now for the ice-hockey final'.

As soon as the match was over he had to dash to another studio to interview Britain's leading woman skier, Addie Pryor, unaware of further embarrassment to come. It was only the third time that a birth had been announced on television, the first was Prince Charles and the second Princess Anne. The press had a field day. The nursing home was besieged and the photograph of baby Marcus and his proud mother in the newspapers was something Liza always treasured.

They engaged a professional nanny, Janet Wiggins, who was to remain with them for five years and as a God-fearing High Anglican, became a great admirer of successive curates at St Anne's church. To meet all these extra costs Liza had to work harder than ever as a freelance. She began writing romantic short stories for *Woman, Woman's Own, Woman's Weekly* and *Woman's Realm*. Articles for *Everybody's*, the *DC Thompson Group*, *The Scotsman*, and in fact, anybody who would have her and, of course, she was still writing for Woody.

Max, too, was busy covering sport for the BBC and the 1956 Melbourne Olympics were imminent but as he was a freelance, he was not included in the BBC team. He was the only commentator who had covered every Olympics since the war so he was determined to work in Melbourne. He wrote to his old boss in the Australian Broadcasting Commission who was now deputy general manager, asking whether he could join their commentary team since he knew they were launching their television service on the strength of the Olympic Games coverage. He got an enthusiastic 'yes' to cover athletics and swimming. Max persuaded Liza that this was an opportunity for husband and wife to work as a team so Liza managed to get commissions from *Woman's Hour* and *Illustrated* and accompanied Max to Australia, leaving me and Marcus in the tender care of Trissie and Nanny.

In 1956 the flight to Australia took four days with overnight stops en route and when they finally arrived, Liza fell for Australia, loving the way that the people were so relaxed and friendly and the wonderful climate. It was such a contrast to the grey, autumnal post-war London that they had left behind.

In Melbourne they 'acquired' a Land Rover which they called Gladys, which they could get to the Olympics every day. The games were opened by the Duke of Edinburgh and he was paying a visit to the British Team when Max and Liza set out to the Olympic Village in Gladys.

Suddenly we realised there were police everywhere and that they were holding back the cheering crowds. Somehow we had got mixed up with the Royal Procession and we couldn't get out of it. What was worse was that we were the fourth car in the royal procession.

'Wave' said Max furiously out of the side of his mouth. I did and got a warm reception, people cheered, the army presented arms and the police saluted! Goodness knows who they thought we were but it got us inside the stadium. I rather enjoyed it, it was extremely funny and rather nerve-wracking. Somehow we managed to disentangle ourselves from the procession once we were inside the grounds. We took refuge with the Singapore Hockey Team. We got away with it but Max had a terrible telling off from his new bosses.

During the Games, Max had become friendly with Stanley Hands, the head of the Australian Film Service, who let them borrow one of his cameras and a cameraman, Frank Bagnall, in order to make a children's television programme. The idea was to stop and film anything or anybody which might interest children in the UK. Frank wasn't keen and obviously felt they were a couple of Pommie amateurs which was quite true. Liza had been in front of the camera a few times but she had no idea how to direct and it was all gloriously haphazard. The plan was to drive as far inland as possible on their way to Sydney in a curve between Melbourne and North Australia.

The first two nights we spent at Tatura Sheep Station. The family were very kind and we got some quite good material, including kangaroos who hopped up quite close to us as if they wanted to know who we were invading their space! On the third day absolutely nothing happened, just flat, baking emptiness. Frank getting more and more bad tempered and I was used as a sort of translator between the two men who wouldn't speak directly to each other.

Daylight was fading when a few ramshackle looking houses appeared, shimmering in the heat. And suddenly we were in the middle of a township. We stopped in front of a veranda where there were four children and a pony. Between them they had a gigantic ice-cream cone. They took it in turns, pony included, to take a lick. Frank forgot his bad temper and jumped out of the Land Rover and set up his camera and just managed to film them before the sun set.

This very small place was called Morundah, the aboriginal name for 'stuck in the mud', which had a population of 130, a great many of whom were children. Next day we asked our kind hosts if were really in the Outback. They smiled at us indulgently.

'Nah – the Outback's over there,' waving to the distant shimmering horizon.

The children talked about their pets and toys and pastimes until we were stopped by a tall thin man who didn't altogether trust us and he removed his son by the ear. There was one star turn, an emu with a wicked pecking beak which walked up and down the street. They had sexed it wrongly and one day she laid an egg. The children had it blown and presented to me.

Max had to return to the Games but Liza got an invitation to visit the Outback.

It was dreamlike to travel by train for mile after mile without seeing a building or a person, although occasionally we were joined by leaping kangaroos. Eventually we reached a very small township with one hotel, one pub and one shop. The people were very friendly and relaxed and some of them were British immigrants hoping to make a new life in Australia. One or two were a bit homesick, but most of them had settled in quite happily with any job they could get. Everybody was very willing to be interviewed on my cumbersome BBC recorder and in the middle of it all I got another shock.

It was an invitation from the Flying Doctor, would I like to join him on a flight? Rather! The next day I was driven by truck to a large warehouse with a landing strip by it. There was nobody about. I was just deposited and the truck drove off. The only thing I could do was to venture into the large, apparently deserted, warehouse where there was one very small aircraft. A man in grimy overalls appeared from behind it and looked at me suspiciously and just went on wiping his hands on a filthy cloth.

'Ever push an aircraft?' he asked suddenly.

Dumbly I shook my head.

'Well now's your chance to learn. Go down that end and shove!'

Slowly the little plane was trundled out into the grilling heat. The doctor drove up out of the heat haze and I tried to explain who I was. His name was Doctor Huxtable and he heard me out and then motioned me on board plus my recorder and overnight bag.

A rather dour-faced pilot called Vic came out to join us. Behind him was a narrow isle and two small seats on either side. He obviously didn't think much of free loaders. Off down the dusty runway we roared and up into the shimmering sky. We flew quite low and again there was this amazing emptiness with kangaroos the only sign of life.

Kind Dr Huxtable shouted into my ear that we had to pick up a jackeroo from a sheep station in the real outback. It wasn't until then that I realised we weren't going to land on a proper air strip. After what seemed a very long time, we banked and began to circle. Far below us was a Land Rover with its radio aerial fully extended with a big handkerchief attached to it. It was driving backwards and forwards very slowly to show the pilot which was the best place to land. I shut my eyes very tightly and put my fingers in my ears as directed by Dr Huxtable and down we went into a remarkably smooth landing. But we still had to reach our ultimate destination. A driver and the Land Rover were waiting for us and we climbed on stiffly and bounced up and down to the Homestead.

A woman came out in the grilling heat. She was very relieved to see Dr Huxtable and led him to the jackeroo's quarters at the back of the building. We were give a cup of scalding hot tea but Vic still wasn't speaking to me much. The patient was carried out in a stretcher. He was a 19 year-old redhead, still wearing a broad-brimmed hat – which he never took off – and he was clutching a pair of long, polished boots. The stretcher was put down in the aisle. Dr Huxtable asked me if I'd talk to the boy who was looking really miserable by now. Somehow I managed to kneel alongside him and to talk and bit by bit he began to relax a little. He'd never been on a plane before and he had never seen a town. Finally he confided his real fear.

'What happens if they let me out of the hospital for a walkabout and I get lost?'

It seemed almost impossible to me in such a small place, but I went on holding his hand and said, 'You just stop a passer-by and ask the way back to the hospital.'

It had never occurred to him and he relaxed visibly and actually managed a grin. Vic actually shook my hand when we landed.

Not long afterwards, when the jackeroo had had his appendix out, he sent me a photograph of himself sitting bolt upright in his hospital bed with a nurse on either side of him. He was still clasping his precious boots.

Vic actually bought me a beer and before I knew what was happening I was invited to a silver mine. This was another great honour and I was taken down 4,000ft to interview two young miners who were just coming off the midnight shift. They were great too and I was really sorry to leave the great emptiness and the amazing friendly people who lived there. All the same, it was a relief to get back to Max and the ending of the Games.

By then it was nearly Christmas and Liza was homesick and missing the children badly. Canberra was their last stop, and its white colonnaded buildings seemed to Liza a real metropolis after the Outback. Max, ever the Great Fixer, had arranged for Liza to interview Dame Patti Menzies, the Prime Minister's wife, who gave a very friendly interview and sent her love to all the children in Britain.

Liza had loved her time in Australia and thought it would have been a marvellous place to bring up children. She tried to persuade Max to move lock stock and barrel but, having done it once, he was not to be persuaded. Had Liza won the argument, the Wombles would have remained undiscovered. However, the trip had provided some invaluable experience for her. 'All of our stuff is written in odd moments,' she wrote to Renée. 'I am sure that it is wonderful training as I have to write articles any time, anywhere, under any conditions.'

Once home, it was back to work with a vengeance. Max being a freelancer it meant their income was definitely shaky at times and there were so many people who were dependent on them – Nanny Janet, Max's very capable and sociable secretary Blue Daniel, whose real name was Constance but she was known to all her friends as 'Blue' because of her wonderful flashing blue eyes, Ann Hockham who helped in the house and the garden, and the rock of the household, Trissie. Her income was exactly £50 a year as she refused to have anything to do with a state pension as it would mean people prying into her affairs. Liza didn't dare tell Max, in fact he never knew, so she had to subsidise her surreptitiously. Trissie's strength was her cooking which was wonderful and she was able to cope with any number of people, often at the last minute, which was just as well as they did a lot of entertaining.

Max was working for all kinds of current affairs programmes as well as sport, both on radio and tv; and work was coming Liza's way from *Woman's Hour* and the *Today* programme which was much more light-hearted then, chaired by Jack de Manio. She was sent to interview all sorts with her BBC recorder, and like all reporters she followed her producer's instructions – which landed her in some strange situations. After a lot of difficulty she managed to get an interview with Gilbert Harding. In the 1950s Harding was a superstar of the media and was constantly hounded by the press, so Liza thought it was very kind of him to give her twenty minutes of his precious time. Unfortunately, it coincided with him having a bath.

The front door was opened by his companion, a charming, long-suffering man who took me as far as the bathroom. He knocked nervously.

'Come in!' yelled Gilbert.

I took a deep breath and, bright red in the face, sidled into the room and sat down on the chair by the bath. Luckily, Gilbert was having a very luxurious bubble bath. Impatiently he waved his sponge at me. I never looked up once and my notebook got rather wet, but at least I'd earned my five guineas.

Harding was gay and somewhat eccentric, so he would have had no deliberate intention of shocking Liza, but – like Winston Churchill, who used to dictate to his secretary when he was in the bath – he used every available minute to get things done and would have given no thought to any female sensibilities. Liza was certainly embarrassed, but it was just the way things were then and she always found it an amusing anecdote.

When she wasn't working for the BBC Liza began her first novel for children, *The Television Mystery* which was largely based on when she and Max were working at BBC Television, Lime Grove, editing their Australian children's film. She sold the idea to publishers Max Parrish. In February 1957 she wrote to Renée,

> My book comes out in six weeks time and they have already sold 500 copies in advance which is good luck. The second should be underway but I haven't got round to it yet, but I can see that when Max gets back he will probably hold me down to the typewriter. He is known as 'The Manager' at *Woman's Hour*!

Max also wrote proudly to his mother:

> I wonder if you heard Liza's talk on *Woman's Hour* the other day. It was done at very short notice and she ad-libbed it most successfully. It was about Australia and I think the producers were most impressed so I hope she will get some more (work). She has been doing a lot of writing since we got back … *The Television Mystery* comes out in a month or so and I hope it has some success for I think it would stir her on to better things.

In fact, *The Television Mystery* was to be the first of nine mystery books for Parrish, in which the main characters were friends Vicky, Peter, Jim and Gappy, who had polio and was confined to a wheelchair. The last was published in 1967.

Six Days to Sydney was transmitted in August 1957, with Max and Liza in the studio doing the live linking. Liza went on writing short stories for women's magazines. *Woman* and *Woman's Own* were the best payers and if they failed she slid down the scale to the cheaper ones; and with luck got £25. She wrote to Renée, 'I've sold another short story and am in *Woman's Weekly, TV Mirror* and *The Scotsman* this week. Variety is the spice of life.' *The Scotsman* newspaper was a favourite of Liza's. 'I've got quite a lot of work on at the moment which is a good thing. My especial joy being the fact that *The Scotsman* have given me a brief to write about anything I like, so I can get few subjects off my chest.' She was also in demand for giving library talks, opening fetes and church bazaars, both as Mrs Max Robertson and in her own right as Elisabeth Beresford.

Max, who had always had an eye for antiques, bought more and more, specialising in Chinese blue and white porcelain, which in the days before the proliferation of television shows on antiques that broadened public knowledge and acquisitiveness, could still be found at bargain prices. It was not unusual for a dealer to turn up in the evening with some china wrapped in newspaper and there would be some hard bargaining over the dinner table. He made some mistakes but he learnt fast, and it did lead to a rather unusual situation. One of his favourite dealers, Evelyn Butler, owned a small antique shop on the Portobello Road and on Saturdays there was a big street market where you could buy just about anything. It was enormously popular and people came from far and wide to visit it. Evelyn rented the strip of pavement in front of the shop to Max. As he invariably covered sport on Saturday for *BBC Grandstand*, Liza had to man the stall.

On Friday night Max would start packing up the china he wanted to sell at the market. It would often take him into the small hours, but early next morning he would load up the car and Liza had to be up, dressed and ready to leave the house at 7am. Max gave Liza a curious code which was an alphabetical equivalent of the price he wanted. Also packed into the car was a card table, cash box and a cloth. Liza recalled that:

Evelyn, who was very kind, kept me supplied with tea throughout the day. I had sandwiches in my pockets and a bag of loose change, usually about five pounds and I was in business. The really important trading was done before 8am when the dealers came round.

'All right, darling. How much is that blue and white vase? Fake of course, and oh dear there's a little crack. Still I'll give you two quid and that's being generous.'

'Three pounds, seven shillings and sixpence,' I said stolidly (having worked out Max's code).

'Tut, tut. Still seeing as how it's you, I'll meet you half way. Two quid.'

'Two pounds fifteen shillings.'

'Well then darling, seeings as its you. Wrap it up for us.'

We both knew that by the time he'd worked his way down the market he would have resold it, probably for a fiver, and made a nice little profit. But as Max had only bought it for 30 shillings it was fair enough.

Business was very brisk for about an hour as the dealers bargained their way through the market, and quite often an object would change hands several times. Then the dealers would vanish, there would be a slight pause and I could at last have my cup of tea and a biscuit. All the real business of the day was over and the general public started to arrive. They were much more tentative and would spend a long time making up their minds. Max stayed well away until the market closed down and I could pack up the few remaining unsold goods. He kept away because he might be recognised from the television.

Following on the success of *Six Days to Sydney* on BBC children's television, Max wanted to do another series. Owen Reid of the BBC was keen and Max decided to produce a film on a more ambitious scale, *Come to the Caribbean*. He found a very good amateur cameraman, Ion Trant, who seemed quite keen on the idea; they had no contract so it was all a gamble. The trip would take five to six weeks in the early spring of 1958 and Max was determined to visit as many islands as possible.

Making all the arrangements took a lot of organisation and they acquired a great deal of equipment. At that time the islands were very unsophisticated and they needed all the publicity they could get to bring in the tourists. Max was away working for BBC Sport so Ion and Liza had to start out on their own on 5 February. Their confidence was shaken from the outset when they were greeted at London Airport with the news that a BEA plane had crashed in Munich, the air disaster in which many of Busby's Babes – the Manchester United football team – perished.

After a diversion to Canada for refuelling and a brief landing in Bermuda, they finally made it to Barbados.

The customs man was foxed by all our equipment and documents. Ion just faded away while I went through the gear and documents over and over again. Finally the customs man gave me a beaming smile, ticked everything and waved us on. Honour was satisfied! We piled our twenty-five pieces of equipment into a taxi and drove to Cacrabanc Hotel. It was right down on the beach with curving yellow sand, turquoise blue sea, crackling palm trees, crimson flower and circling snow white doves.

The next morning we went in to Bridgetown to see about hiring a Land Rover but we couldn't get any help at all. Everybody smiled and talked to us in their soft voices. Everywhere there were donkey carts and sauntering, chattering women with big bundles on their heads. We were taken out to lunch on the east of the island and Ion managed to film the flying fish arriving and a small girl to carry the continuity board while I splashed in to record some of the fishermen. We went on to Sam Lord's Castle which was white, shaded, and somehow still sinister long after his infamous buccaneering ways. The islanders all told us 'He was a BAD man!'

The 'ex-pat' community sometimes grated with Liza. The 'club' atmosphere and the insistence on serving up Sunday roasts as if they were in England rather than on a tropical island.

A planter invited us for a drink on his plantation and then we were driven back to the Cacrabanc by a chauffeur. Bernard Moore of the BBC Overseas Service was there and everybody droned on and, of course, it was roast beef. Ion and I both wanted to sleep and sleep but we dragged ourselves off to go and film the children in their starched

Sunday best and then down to Rockley Beach where we filmed a steel band.

The next stop was Trinidad where Max caught up with them at the Tate & Lyle sugar factory. Wherever the trio went, they were met with great hospitality and friendliness. Liza's main task was continuity and note-taking which was almost impossible in the heat, but there was always the longed-for swim at the end of the day and a planter's punch or two to keep her hydrated and happy. As they island-hopped, filming the people and the beautiful scenery, Liza had to ensure that the twenty-six pieces of luggage and equipment went with them – which was no mean feat.

In British Guiana (Belize) Liza had a close brush with nature in the raw.

There was a small group of sightseers and an Amerindian guide who materialised out of the great, dark jungle. He was carrying an enormous rifle which must have been a real antique. God knows if it worked. We set out in single file and as I was the only woman I was placed in the middle. It was a very rough track and the jungle began to close in round us. We were held up by monkeys swinging out of the jungle and leaping from tree to tree to cross over the track. They hurled insults at us and vanished into the darkness. We stepped over a line of busy leaf-cutting ants and our guide suddenly held up his hand. We stopped, hardly daring to breathe, as out of the darkness slithered an enormous 20ft anaconda. It took no notice of us as it carried on its silent way, crossing the track in front of us and vanished into the jungle. Even more unnerving was to hear the roar of the Kaieteur Falls as we emerged into the grilling heat of daylight. The great Potaro River seemed to flow quite slowly out of the jungle and then gathered speed until the water poured down the Falls, dropping 740ft to created a racing white cloud of foam over which a complete circular rainbow danced and shivered.

In Grenada which was suffocatingly hot, Liza was sitting on the kerb, writing in her continuity notebook when she was joined by a very old islander. 'He took a swig of rum out of a bottle, smiled at me and died. The police were very efficient at taking away the body.' Their final stop was the tiny island of Bequia, where they borrowed a rusty old jeep and a driver. It was election time and the driver had a Tannoy fixed to the car; as they bounced and thumped round the coastline he kept up his election cry, even stopping to harangue a goat which ambled across the road in front of them. 'Come out and vote!' he bellowed at the bewildered animal.

Having filmed and interviewed their way across the islands, visiting banana and sugar plantations, the nutmeg industry in Grenada, the sea-island cotton in St Vincent, beaches and other tourist spots, it was time to think of returning home. Jamaica was their last stop where, after dinner at the Residency, Liza was typing out a shot list in the bedroom of their hotel. The West Indies had one last surprise in store.

> There was a noise like an underground train roaring past. Everything tilted slightly and my precious typewriter slid down the table. I just managed to catch it before it hit the floor and went on typing.
>
> 'What was that?!' Max shot up from his bed where he had been dozing.
>
> 'Earthquake,' I said briefly and got on with typing up my notes.

The producer at Lime Grove was her priority. She had to become an expert on linking, and a studio in Wardour Street where all the films were cut became her second home. At the same time she was trying to fit in writing and a new, regular job for BBC TV, chairing *Mainly for Women*, a domestic forum in which viewers' questions were discussed spontaneously by a panel.

The film was to be Max and Liza's last collaborative television adventure. The eight episodes were popular with their young audience, but the days of amateur film crews were passing and the BBC was not willing to fund further Robertson adventures in the Commonwealth. Max's commentating skills were being put to good use by BBC Sport and Liza was firmly tied to her typewriter, concentrating increasingly on children's books and children's television drama.

In 1957, she began writing mystery thrillers for children's television: a children's six-part television drama for Associated Rediffusion Television (ATV), the first commercial franchise television company which began transmission in 1955. Called *The Chinese Dagger*, it drew on Liza's experience of auctions with Max. This was followed by *McFarlane's Way*, also a six-parter, based on a lonely Scottish island called Craigie (and the cast included a character called 'Morse'!). The two main young protagonists were reunited in her next mystery serial which was aimed more at young teenagers, *The Diamond Bird*. Then came *The Old Pull 'n Push* (1959) in which children save a branch line from closing. This proved highly popular so a sequel was commissioned, *The Return of the Old Pull n' Push* (1961). Liza enjoyed the challenge of writing the serials and in a letter to her mother-in-law reported that, '[*The Old Pull n' Push*] has had some good write-ups in the daily press and seems to be going well ... they are telerecording it so that means there are hopes of its being sold overseas. The first time such a deal will have been considered, so I'm a pioneer!' but grumbled about the budget limitations in her diary:

> The mean budget only allows four sets per episode and a minimum of characters ... It entails lots of staring into the mid-distance while my brain works out plot and counterplot like an adding machine. Only twenty guineas an instalment which is real hack writing ... I like writing dialogue but just don't know how it will act. Have to do all the parts myself in turn ... this writing business is very exhausting.

The occasional film review for Woody meant an escape from the tyranny of domestic pressures but she knew she had to make best use of her talents in children's literature.

> It was a relief to to write children's books ... The advance was £50 out of which my agent got a fiver. I was writing all kinds of adventures, many of them based on my work and travels. My favourites were the magic books. You could go anywhere, even back in time, and I was allowed a pretty free hand by the publishers, and I started getting royalties ... but it was an endless grind producing more and more articles and short stories as well as doing reports for BBC Radio.

Liza's magic books were arguably her best creations; where her imagination could roam and her penchant for jokes be indulged. As a child she had loved Edith Nesbitt, perhaps best remembered today as the author of *The Railway Children*, but her stories of magical adventures – *Five Children and It, The Phoenix and the Carpet* and *The Story of the Amulet* – made a great impression on the young Liza, tucked away in her bedroom in

Brighton in the 1930s. Rather than Nesbitt's family-centred books, Liza's magic books tended to have lonely children at their heart, a theme so brilliantly developed by J.K. Rowling decades later, and she, too, has humour at the core of her books. Liza's love of history was put to good use when her characters travelled back in time and in *Awkward Magic* (Rupert Hart Davies 1964) there is a sniff of things to come where she dwells on air pollution and overcrowding. The magic creature at the heart of this tale, set in Brighton, is a griffin, and he sums up Liza's philosophy: 'There's plenty of magic about if you keep your eyes open for it. Now you've got a taste for it you'll probably spot the odd charm or spell, or something, all over the place. Only do, for goodness sake, be careful. It's quite strong some of it.'

However, both domestic and work life were not without their funny moments. Liza covered the spectrum when she interviewed people for radio and magazines. The 13th Duke of Bedford was opening Woburn Abbey to the public for the first time and Liza was sent by BBC Radio to interview him.

I drove my Mini down the great drive with deer grazing on either side and was greeted by the butler, who obviously thought I should have gone round to the tradesman's entrance. As I was unloading all my gear, the Duke came bounding across the great hall.

He was a lovely man, down to earth, and he needed all the publicity he could get. What I didn't know was that he had recently acquired a new woman in his life, shortly to become his duchess. She was a suspicious and jealous Frenchwoman. We had no sooner begun the recording in one of the palatial rooms than she caught on that the Duke had a female visitor. She threw open the great doors with a crash.

'Ooo is that woman?' She demanded.

'Run!' Whispered the Duke. Clutching the microphone I obeyed his orders. Through the Abbey we cantered with him still expanding on the beauties of his home. I panted alongside him with questions, pursued by the Frenchwoman. By some miracle the interview was perfectly okay, if a bit breathless, and he got the publicity he so richly deserved. I always had a very soft spot for him.

There was another ridiculous occasion when she was sent by the Central Office of Information to interview the ravens in the Tower of London.

> I did several interviews with a very nice guide and everything went very smoothly until I remembered I was supposed to get a recording of the famous ravens. I felt rather at a loss and then I caught a glimpse of the large, black-feathered birds who were pecking away at the grass in a small enclosure. I looked round but there was nobody in sight so I clambered over the restraining rope and approached them slowly so as not to frighten them away. They backed up a little nervously but went on pecking. I went down on my knees, switched on the recorder and held the microphone towards them. The birds looked at me sideways and went on pecking.
>
> I was desperate. Perhaps I could encourage them? I cleared my throat and tried to make some encouraging, raven-like noises. The birds retreated a bit and desperately I tried again.
>
> 'Caw, caw, caw, CAW!'
>
> No response. I gave up, turned off the recorder and got stiffly to my feet. I'd been so engrossed in what I was trying to do, I'd been oblivious to everything else. Pressed against the ropes were a whole lot of tourists, their cameras clicking and obviously entranced by this mad woman.
>
> I fled back to the COI and handed my tapes to the editor with my notes. Some time later when I was doing another job for the COI, the recording engineer, Alan, stopped me in the corridor.
>
> 'That recording you did of the ravens in the Tower of London is first class, Liza, and the BBC has asked to borrow it from archives...'

As the 1950s drew to a close, magic was in short supply in Liza's life. She was always busy, always writing, but unable by her own admission to raise her eyes from the typewriter to see the bigger picture. She was still worrying about money, but less about her own ability to meet the demands that life threw at her. She was working as a journalist for several television and radio programmes – *Topic, Woman's World, Woman's Hour* – as well as writing children's books, romantic short stories and she had embarked on her first romantic novel. I was at a local preparatory school and Marcus began his schooling at a local pre-prep. Nanny Janet moved on and a series of Dutch *au pairs* moved in in her stead. Without really thinking about it, Liza was a successful, working mother which was not necessarily viewed as a Good Thing by other wives. She received a very formal invitation for coffee from one of the other (well-known) commentator's wives who lived in St John's Wood.

As usual I was very short of time but I didn't want to let Max down so I went. Coffee was served rather formally in the drawing-room and my hostess hummed and hawed a bit until she finally came to the point.

'Elisabeth, the others commentators' wives in the Department have asked me to tell you that we think you're letting us down by going out to work. It makes us look as if we need money.'

I was totally devoid of speech. I gabbled an excuse and left. I never told Max or Mother. I hate to think what their reactions would have been.

Liza thought she was failing as a writer and a wife, but with hindsight it is fairly clear that she was being undermined by the implacable forces of Max and Mother. Max was a very complex character, on the one hand very driven and on the other naive; he could be very selfish, his childhood had taught him self-preservation and he thought that his plans and ambitions were pre-eminent. Liza could see the flaws and was horrified by his ability to 'fritter' money away. Summing up in her diary at the end of 1958, she wrote:

Odd points come to mind. Max's sudden, unexpected slip downhill, physically and morally at the end of the year. He had spent over £1,000 on blue china and I had warnings ringing in my ears. But what can I do – he isn't a man with whom you can reason in any way. Common sense is not his and whatever he touches turns to dross. But is it his fault? ... He just isn't easy to work with and he gets ideas – grand and lofty – and then fails to push them through.

Very fairly, she sifts the evidence to see if it is her fault and her lack of confidence is evident.

Each time I come to the conclusion I really will help him every way I can, he annihilates all loyalty by some silly action. I'm not big enough to over-ride such obstacles. I know I'm small in my way. I've never done a large thing in my life and never will. I'm a middle-way plodder without much vision and spend my time avoiding difficult issues ... The trouble with most of us Englishwomen is that we don't develop until we are in our 30s and then it is too late.

The two travel films for the BBC had opened up a difference between them: Liza learned to cut, edit and do live links and was deeply involved in the process; she was equal in the partnership but Max had not acknowledged this, nor perhaps understood how much the two projects had relied on her input. With her children's books, radio work and journalism, her star was in the ascendancy.

Chapter 5

In Demand

For Liza, the Sixties were to prove transformational: she discovered the island of Alderney, wrote her first romantic novel, began a long and happy association with the Central Office of Information and, most importantly, wrote her most enduring children's book, *The Wombles*.

In the previous decade she had enjoyed increasing employment as what she called 'a hack', both as a trade, radio and occasional TV journalist and a writer of romantic fiction for women's magazines. She had also embarked on children's television serials and by 1960 had five children's books published. Gradually the balance began to tip: the journalism diminished and the children's fiction blossomed. Her perennial worry about money was still at the core of every key she bashed on her 'tryper', and she made weekly visits to the Westminster Bank at Bellevue Road, Wandsworth Common, to check her balance and, if it had been a good week, deposit cheques. More often or not there were cries of 'none of the sewers are paying me!' The BBC paid five guineas for a radio piece which would involve research, driving up to Broadcasting House to pick up the recorder, driving on to the interviewee – which could be anywhere, and then back to BH to return the recorder and do the studio links. 'They are a mean bunch,' she would say, 'I flog my guts out for a measly five guineas.'

Domestic pressure remained unabated too. Max was covering a wide variety of Outside Broadcasts for *Grandstand*, including swimming, athletics and winter sports, which meant he was away a great deal. On his return, there were would be a flourish of activity before the next job in which Liza was expected to engage fully, regardless of her work – and the fact that he had a secretary. Then he would be off again, Liza often accompanying him to the airport bus terminal in the Cromwell Road, shorthand notebook in hand as he reeled off instructions. Max's interest in Chinese blue-and-white porcelain had not abated, in fact it was to stand him in good stead when he was approached to be the chairman of *Going for a Song*, the first television series to be devoted to antiques. In the Fifties Liza had accompanied him on many antiquing jaunts which had often caused her despair, although she always enjoyed the trips away from the pressures of home life, either domestic or abroad to places like Switzerland and the South of France. That was a pattern which was to change when Alan and Renée could no longer cope with the exigencies of farming life and a large house. By 1962 they were aged 79 and 71 respectively and they planned to sell Gibbet Oak and move to a bungalow near their daughter Marian and her husband, retired tea planter Bob Carswell, who lived near Dedham, Essex.

Liza, Marcus and I very occasionally joined by Max, had enjoyed wonderful family holidays at Gibbet Oak. There, we children could roam happily without being watched over – climb trees, explore the woods, go riding at the nearby stables run by the appropriately named Miss Mount, play clock golf and French cricket – all the activities which were impossible in London. Max and Liza would go off, leaving Marcus and me with Gran-gran and Grandfather. How could this wonderful sort of escapist holiday be replicated? I was due to start at boarding school that autumn and Marcus was making great headway at his pre-prep, so Liza was desperate to find somewhere we could have a memorable summer holiday.

The answer came from an unexpected quarter and was to be a life-changing decision. Peter Seabourne, a television director friend, offered his holiday cottage on the Island of Alderney. Liza, thinking that must be somewhere off the Scottish coast and with happy memories of her hitching days in the WRNS, grabbed at this generous lifeline and the deed was done. She always said that it was only when the Heron aeroplane from Gatwick flew south to the Channel Islands that she realised how wrong she was.

The holiday 'gang' consisted of Liza, Blue Daniel, our Dutch *au pair* Lies Krapp, and we children. The Heron landed on what Liza called 'a small rock in the middle of the sea', and rather in the mould of Mrs Durrell, she gathered up her resolve and her gang and decamped to the Seabourne house, a white-washed cottage in a terrace of similar, stone-built houses on a charming cobbled street in the 'town' of St Anne. The walls were thick, the diamond-paned windows small and the ceilings low. A little garden led down some steps to a gate which opened up onto Connaught Square, and to the right was the Connaught Hotel, to the

left the Island Hall. Even to childish eyes everything seemed smaller and
older somehow, and to London eyes, utterly charming.

Seventeen years earlier, Alderney had been a very different island. When
it became obvious in 1940 that the Germans would invade the Channel
Islands, the islanders decided to evacuate and upped sticks to Glasgow.
The Germans spent the next three years fortifying the island with gun
emplacements, pill boxes and a sea wall because of its strategic importance
in the Channel, just over seven miles from mainland France. To do this
they imported slave labour, including Russians and French, who were
kept in two camps. The majority of these men died from exhaustion and
undernourishment. When the islanders returned in 1945, they found their
homes ravaged and barely standing; there was no sign of life, no livestock,
pets, even the birds had gone. With true islander grit they set about
restoring their homes, their lives and the natural beauty of Alderney.

Gradually normality returned and breathed new life into the 3½ x
1½ mile 'rock', so that by the time we first landed there it was a holiday
heaven. We all succumbed to its magic, the sandy beaches, turquoise sea,
and mysterious cliffs. For Liza it was a godsend. She did not have to
worry about Marcus and me, happy to let us roam. There was no nagging
telephone in the house, the peace was almost perfect as in those days there
were few cars on the island and we walked everywhere. Lunch would be a
picnic on a beach, where we swam in the icy cold sea which, depending on
the beach we went to was either pellucid or churning rollers which were
brilliant for body surfing. Liza was a strong swimmer and her love of the
sea had never diminished and she would swim from bay to bay doing lazy
backstroke. Sometimes a sea fret would roll in, almost without warning
and so thick that the temperature would drop. Then the lighthouse would
start its mournful 'ooooerumph', sounding like a lost dinosaur, and Danny
and the island bus would appear as if summoned by magic through the
gloom to scoop us all up.

That first summer holiday of two weeks nourished Liza's soul and
renewed and fed her imagination. It set the pattern for years to come,
extending to four weeks in the summer and then a week or so at Easter as
well. On that first visit, Liza recorded in her diary:

A blazing day. Lies and I gave the house a turn-out – sand everywhere
and in everything – while Blue did the shopping. We rolled off to

Braye (beach) and lay in the dunes baking while the wind ruffled the grass and the sea was blue as sapphires. We went in – oh it was cold – then slowly one's breath came back in great gasps … It was really wonderful and we were all burning like sausages under the grill as we went up to the pub for a drink and then came home.

During that first visit in 1962, Max paid Alderney a brief visit. Beaches were of no interest to him and there were no antique shops to browse so he investigated the possibility of buying a property. It set Liza's teeth on edge, she could not see beyond her hard-earned money being frittered away and the added responsibility; her tranquillity was spoiled momentarily. Three days later, Max flew off again in a flurry of instructions as to whom she should contact to view properties, but Liza did her usual trick of prevaricating and buried her head in the sand. Nothing more was said.

Liza may, instead, have been thinking of her new editor, John Denton at Ernest Benn, and his suggestion that she should write for a new series of books which he was commissioning, under the imprint of Friday Press. She had sent a synopsis for *The Mulberry Street Team* to Ernest Benn at the suggestion of her agent, Osyth Leeston of A.M. Heath. Osyth was one of the great agents for children's writers, having represented Noel Streatfield, Judith Kerr and Joan Aiken among other luminaries of children's literature. She recognised good storytellers and nurtured them. In her diary of 24 July, 1962, she wrote:

Drove to meet Mr Denton of Ernest Benns at the Royal Court Hotel. He was smallish, nervous, shy, bespectacled, keen. He wanted to make changes but was quite polite about most of the stuff and I suddenly saw a whole new firm – Friday Books – with me. Dead scared I was, but had the sense not to let on. Oh dear, oh dear, Still, I'll do my best.

As it transpired, Liza only wrote two books for the Friday imprint, *A Holiday for Slippy* being the second but Denton was to have other ideas in store for her. Meanwhile she kept pounding away at her tryper.

I seemed to disappear under a great flood tide of work and am only now seeing daylight for a few minutes! Not that I mind, I'm delighted, but it did get a bit much for a while. I finished a 22,000 word stint at 10.30 last night and have been out since early this morning to do a recording for Today. It was quite fun but it meant going down to the East End in the pouring rain.

During the early part of the decade, as the Beatles helped to shake off the grey post-war world and heralded a brighter future, further new opportunities were coming Liza's way. She was offered a job as head of the children's script department for a commercial TV company. 'Two thousand pounds a year and expenses,' she crowed, 'but I don't want to work away from home and so asked for more money and shorter hours to put them off. I think I must have succeeded as they haven't called back.'

Liza was in greater demand than she gave herself credit for. The magic titles were increasingly popular: *Two Gold Dolphins* (Constable 1961) was her first book to sell in the American market, followed by *Awkward Magic* (Constable 1964), published in the United States in 1965 under the title *The Magic World*. *Awkward Magic* brings to life her childhood in Kemp Town: Joe finds a stray dog which turns out to be a griffin and they embark on a treasure hunt. Interestingly, the griffin, which has travelled from the ancient world, is very shocked by the air pollution and over-crowding. This was the first intimation in Liza's writing of her environmental awareness.

With a number of reprints and successes under her belt, she felt able to indulge her long-held aspiration to write a romantic novel. She had written hundreds of romantic short stories for women's magazines but she wanted to develop the story beyond 2,000 words. In 1963, *Paradise Island* was published by Robert Hale, the first of fourteen titles she wrote over the next twenty years. They were sheer escapism and she loved writing them. In the last two years of her life she read and reread them constantly as they provoked happy memories and an escape from her hospital bed. By the late 1960s she was involved in the Romantic Novelists Association which was only founded in 1960 by such luminaries as Barbara Cartland, Rosamunde Pilcher and Catherine Cookson. Liza loathed the committee work but enjoyed the lunches.

The early 1960s also saw the start of another pie into which Liza put her finger with relish, the Central Office of Information. This was an executive agency of the government formed in 1946 as a successor to the Ministry of Information, which promoted British industry and products around the world, propaganda of the mildest and inoffensive kind. It produced public information films and radio programmes on a wide and diverse range of topics. The COI was based in Vauxhall, near Waterloo Station, and was a near neighbour of MI6 in its old office in Hercules Rd. Liza's great friend and colleague Gladdie had migrated to the COI from the Conservative Central Office and suggested that Liza should freelance for them as a journalist and broadcaster. She leapt at the chance and her association with the COI over the following ten years brought her wonderful friendships and a much-needed steady income.

In charge of her office was Conn Ryan, a charming and erudite Irishman, married to a BBC drama producer, Anne; Chrissie Griffiths, a Liverpudlian producer who became one of Liza's greatest friends; Pat Wallace who, among other things, had played the Wurlitzer organ at the Granada Clapham Junction; David Turner, and many more technicians and engineers, joined a few years later by Ivor Mills, former ITN newsreader and heartthrob. What they all had in common, in addition to professionalism and talent, was a wicked sense of humour. Liza had not really worked in a team since her days as a Wren and the camaraderie and fun she had at the COI kept her grounded. The office also had the added bonus of a bird's eye view of all the railway lines converging on Waterloo, so in the school holidays she was able to take Marcus, who had inherited his grandfather's interest in steam trains, to the office where he sat glued to the window, watching and noting the numbers of trains.

This steady income, which usually involved spending a day a week in the office, and more hours out on the hunt for interviews and copy, plus royalties from an increasing number of published books, gave Liza the confidence and wherewithal to buy a house in Alderney. This was to be her bolthole and eventually her full-time residence, but when she viewed it in 1965 it was very basic and she felt very uncertain as to whether it was the right thing to do. It was an eighteenth-century worker's cottage built of stone on three floors with the immensely thick walls typical of the island, situated on a cobbled street at the very top of the town of St Anne. It wasn't so many years before that when cows from nearby fields had overwintered on the ground floor. The rear garden was raised ten feet above street level and looked straight out across neighbouring gardens, towards the southern cliffs.

It was in fear and trepidation that Liza had asked Hoskins & Herivel, estate agents for details of a potential purchase. Commander Hoskins, who had an aura of high naval competence and a jolly twinkle but had, it was rumoured, actually commanded a riverboat in East Africa, produced property details. In her diary for 23 August 1965 she wrote:

> I went to see the dapper little Commander – we hedged a bit: they have had a bad year, the squeeze is definitely on – he gave us some addresses but oddly we picked a wrong house – and rather liked it. Hardly furnished, bleak and base, but large and old with a garden. Saw another – much grander – but smaller.
>
> Damned if I know what to do. Wish now that I hadn't embarked on the whole business. Am prevaricating like mad ... talked to the man next door and he said he was a builder and offered to look over the house for me. Anyway we all went round it and I think the children liked it. What shall I do? ... To take a tremendous step like this needs more backbone than I possess.

Liza took advice from her stockbroker and friends and eventually took the leap in September, purchasing 22 Little Street for the princely sum of £2,000. The decision to buy a house with her own money, far from home, continued to prey on her mind for several years, but despite all the worries she grew to love it.

It was in the mid-Sixties that she found herself in greater demand with publishers. She was writing children's books for Friday Books (Ernest Benn), Methuen, Hart-Davis and Max Parrish; romantic fiction for Robert Hale; and career books for Collins. In addition, she had her COI works, magazine articles and regular contributions to *The Scotsman* newspaper. She began using Gladdie's flat in Balham as a bolthole where she could work uninterrupted by Max, mother and domestic life. In 1964, Max had begun his thirteen-year tenure as chairman of *Going For A Song*, the BBC TV panel game where celebrity guests had to guess the worth of antiques brought before them and experts – most notably Arthur Negus – described the objects and gave more accurate valuations. This was recorded in the studio at BBC Bristol which meant that Max was away for a couple of nights a week and he once again became a recognised 'face', which did his ego an enormous amount of good.

John Denton, Liza's editor at Ernest Benn, dropped the Friday Books imprint and Liza found herself working directly for Ernest Benn. The first title was *The Hidden Mill* (1965), a very naturalistic story about three street-wise children who find an abandoned mill on a south London river, a thinly disguised Wandle, a small tributary of the Thames which meanders through Wandsworth and which, in the eighteenth century, was peppered with paper mills. It was probably the book of which she was most proud. This was followed by a learning-to-read picture book translated into phonics, *Peter Climbs a Tree* (Peeter Clims a Tree) for Ernest Benn in 1966, and at a meeting with Denton and her agent Osyth Leeston, on 8 December, discussions led to a new book which was to change Liza's life.

> Lunch with Osyth and John Denton – good and filling – and he told me 'Peeter' had sold 10,000 for which I receive ... £45 ... He wants me to find the answer to the 'Paddington' series and that my jolly boys is easier said (than done) ... So there it is – lucky me with work commissioned and not an idea in my head.

Ten days after this lunch, with Christmas looming and the prospect of elderly relatives coming to stay, Liza bundled Marcus and me into her minivan and we drove to Wimbledon Common for some fresh air and time away from the all-pervasive Christmas preparations. She parked at the Windmill, a wonderful landmark with its Dutch-style sails which has stood sentinel on the Common since 1817, and then we ran exuberantly down to the Queensmere (lake) where, in the excitement of it all, I called out in Spoonerish style, 'Isn't it marvellous on Wombledon Cimmon!' Liza had an epiphany as her fertile mind went into overdrive. 'That's it!' she exclaimed, 'Wombles!'

The Common provided a wonderful natural world for Liza's imagination to inhabit with over 1,000 acres of woods, open land and nine ponds a few miles south of central London. Here, wildlife and people enjoy a haven of peace and delight away from the hustle and bustle of a capital city. Sadly, wherever there are people there is rubbish, keeping the Common Rangers constantly busy clearing up after visitors. But what if they had secret helpers, and not only secret but whose great purpose in life was to turn the rubbish into practical good use?

That evening she recorded in her diary: 'We had a wonderful time in the morning up on Wimbledon Common and I think I'll invent a new race called "The Wombles". They are in my head, rather like tubby little bats – there's something there.' At a later date she recalled that, 'As soon as I got home I typed out a list of Womble characters taking their names out of the old atlas which belonged to my grandfather 100 years ago.'

Her nascent idea was put on the back burner until March as she was working on *The Island Bus* for Methuen. She wrote two chapters and sent if off to Osyth and Methuen and cleared the decks.

March 13th: It really is difficult when you get to the bit where you have to launch yourself off into space again. I got down to The Wombles ... think they could be good – very good creation – but it's completely new ground for me.

March 14th: Back to The Wombles. It was great fun to do but pretty hard slog and by the time I'd finished I felt pretty whacked.

March 30th: John Denton told me how enthusiastic they were for The Wombles. Had a satisfying picture of Uncle Bulgaria suddenly calling at the end of the board meeting 'One moment, gentlemen...'

After this promising start she had to turn her attention to other commitments such as the next Methuen book and the COI. It was not until October, and with some reluctance, that she returned to the Wombles; like a jittery racehorse at the starting post, she had set off at a gallop but could not jump the first hurdle. She recorded her despair in her diary:

I cannot get those Wombles off the ground – shall try again later. Do hope that some of the stuff in fiction I'm writing now will be ok. If it weren't for the COI I should be dead ... I cannot, CANNOT get on with that book, it makes me feel guilty clean through ... So hard to start on The Wombles AGAIN and managed about two pages, then had to pack up.

Then came the breakthrough on 20th October: 'Got down to The Wombles and by some miracle they started to come good. I battled on like

mad, had the first chapter under my belt and then fell out to the garden …
oh so relieved – although I still don't know whether it'll be ok.'

A month later she is still showing hesitancy: 'No matter how hard I
work at pieces like this (*The Scotsman*) I still feel guilty because I'm not
Wombling, I suppose I'm frightened of them.'

Finally, Liza decided that the distractions of home and non-Womble
writing jobs were too much to bear. Marcus and I were both at boarding
schools in Broadstairs and she, feeling the pull of the sea and the attraction
of a change of scene, booked herself into the Castlemaine Hotel situated
on the front between Broadstairs and Duncton Gap. She spent a week
there in November seeing us at the weekends and completing the first
Wombles book in her hotel bedroom. On Monday 27 November she
recorded:

How strange it is to wake up and realise the day is entirely your own
– not a very attractive day to be sure – but all mine and the Wombles
… How slowly we moved, the Wombles and I … had lunch and once
more returned to it and slowly, very slowly began to pick up speed …
Think I have done only some 7–8,000 words. They are <u>quite</u> good.
Once the thing is a whole perhaps I shall be able to shape it.

The following day, after walking into Broadstairs for a breath of fresh air
and returning Marcus and two friends who broke out of school in search
of a game of cards with her, she returned to her typewriter. 'Poured myself
out a large drink – had dinner – and kept pouring, I went on and on in a
kind of wild frenzy until nearly midnight … realised blearily that I had
written 12,000 words.'

Finally, on the evening of Wednesday the 29th: 'To work once more,
removing myself to the deserted lounge as the rest of the hotel began to
sleep about me and at half past midnight I was done, DONE. Read some
of it sprawled across my bed – it's there – I think.'

As with Charles Dickens, Broadstairs – old-fashioned and cut off from
the hubbub of city life, with its bracing sea air – had reinvigorated Liza's
imagination. The Wombles were born.

The first book introduced the main characters who lived in a burrow on
Wimbledon Common. Liza had no real idea of what they looked like,

more teddy bear than the snout-nosed Wombles which emerged later, but she knew each of them very well because they were all based on members of her family. They were naturally gregarious, living in a structured society ruled over by the patriarch, Great Uncle Coburg Bulgaria, based on her kind but strict father-in-law. 'GUB' as she used to refer to him, was over 300 years old, wore a tartan shawl and spectacles, and the first duty of any Womble going to clear up litter on the common was to find him a discarded copy of *The Times* newspaper. If there was any danger to face, young Wombles went for comfort and sound advice to GUB, normally to be found in his study. It was here that young Wombles graduating from the Womblegarten went to pick their names from the ancient atlas. Although Liza was a feminist in the loosest definition of the word, the cooking (all vegetarian) was the province of Madame Cholet who could rustle up blackberry or dandelion pie to feed the hungriest of Wombles, did not suffer fools gladly and ruled her kitchen fiercely. She was Trissie, Liza's indomitable mother. The third 'adult' Womble was Tobermory, who was based on Liza's middle brother Aden. He spends most of his time in his recycling workshop making ingenious and useful gadgets out of the objects the young Wombles find on the Common. The principal young Wombles were Orinoco (son Marcus), Bungo (me), Wellington (nephew John) and Tomsk (Eleanor Craxton, daughter of one of Liza's best friends). Everyone morning come rain or sun, the young Wombles were out on the Common picking up rubbish and putting it into their tidy bags to take back to the burrow. In the course of this environmental activity they had adventures. 'Human Beings' failed to see them on the whole, but the occasional dog could cause a problem.

Following the completion of the manuscript, Liza waited for the plummeting depression which was her usual reaction to finishing a book but instead, when Max joined her on the Friday, she developed a temperature and on Saturday morning caught the train back to London, clutching her tryper and manuscript, missing my school play and the remainder of the weekend in Broadstairs.

On 21 December, Liza received an early Christmas present when she went to see John Denton at Benn's and he said they would be publishing the book. 'He was really enthusiastic Womblewise. But really, I was so surprised I hardly registered it.'

As it happened, *The Wombles* surpassed even her imaginings and were to change her life for ever – but not just yet, as she returned to her usual full-pelt work for the COI's *Woman's World*, BBC jobs and writing children's and romantic books and articles. Work was never dull.

There were some interviewees who had to be coaxed and wheedled into saying anything at all. Interviewing for *Woman's Hour* at Kew Gardens was just one such example when Liza and her BBC colleagues ended up with hours of recording which were an editing nightmare.

We started off with a cracking interview with the head gardener of the Succulent House who had one plant over 100 years old. From then on our interviewees tapered off. The Rock Garden keeper was dull, another was Bolshie and the old woman who keeps the index references was mad and had to be calmed and coaxed. A scientific student said 'um' every other word, two scientists preached, and a gate keeper was definitely rude!

1967 also yielded its fair share of celebrity interviews.

Drove to the Granada, Tooting (to interview Engelbert Humperdinck). It was quite incredible. Humperdinck was on the bill and the Walker Brothers. The teenagers were screaming – mob hysteria – it took four large men to detach one girl from a singer. They cry hysterically, go rigid, wet their seats, tear off their clothes. My God, it was terrifying and somehow unbearably pathetic … those desperate, raving haunted faces. With an escort I got down under the stage to interview the man: thin, sweating, covered in orange make-up. He gave quite a good interview, somehow unreal. I was glad to escape home to peace and tranquillity.

Two days later she had a very different experience of stardom when she went to interview Val Doonican, the Irish crooner and television personality, for the COI, 'He was extremely nice, very natural and wonderfully talkative. Oh what a splendid man,' she wrote.

Cilla Black was another easy and professional interviewee whom Liza found intelligent, lively and a wonderful talker; Ken Dodd, interviewed at the Palladium, was very funny and gave a 'good piece'; but Rolf Harris was 'extremely depressed and obviously quite exhausted so I got rather a sad interview with him'. Sometimes – and this was before the days of celebrity press conferences in hotels – there would be other journalists present at an interview. One such was an interview with Anthony Newley, then married to Joan Collins, at their home in Hampstead.

> The flat was large, untidy and there were childish voices in the background. The au pair girl sat us down and soon a rather superior young man from *The Sunday Times* arrived. 'Who do these actors think they are?' he said as we waited.
>
> 'Colour supplement?' I asked.
>
> 'No, Atticus' he replied crushingly. Another and splendid young man was complaining plaintively about lugging boxes and calling out 'Joanie, I've got your wigs for tonight.' And, at last, Mr Newley appeared. Spruce, moustached, with dark blue eyes and a sad manner. He warmed slowly to the interview, watched superciliously by Atticus.

Panel games could have provided another string to Liza's bow but they shot an arrow through her Achilles tendon instead. Max was chairing a BBC Radio panel game produced by David Hatch called *Tennis Elbow Foot Game*. She went to see a recording which she found 'Very funny – guest star was Beverley Nicholls, larger and more charming than I'd imagined and Dickie Murdoch, a burnt-out case.' Perhaps this gave her the courage to say 'yes' to an invitation to appear as a panellist on *Just A Minute*, the radio quiz which requires participants to talk about a subject for sixty seconds without repetition, hesitation or deviation, almost as impossible as trying to eat a doughnut without licking your lips. It had only started the previous year but proved to be very popular and continues to this day. Fellow panellists included actress Betty Marsden who was 'very nervous and sick twice', Clement Freud 'aloof', and 'a small, pale girl called Carol Binstead, who obviously hated me for some reason'.

'Later, with good reason, I hated myself. I was diabolically bad. We were on the second recording and everyone, audience included, was exhausted. I crept away and went home in the calm of despair.'

For once, her self-criticism was correct, she was not invited to take part again.

Having delivered the first Wombles manuscript to John Denton, Liza was writing for Hart-Davies, Methuen, and Robert Hale as well as other children's books for Benns. Her latest romantic novel, *A Tropical Affair*, was published on 22 May, and a day later her third magic book, *Sea Green Magic*. By the end of 1968 Liza felt more secure about money. She had a lot of work and her income had begun to take off. Her romantic novels began to sell overseas and she also had a breakthrough with the *Learning to Read* books. 'Children in America and Europe are going to learn their letters from my books. Ridiculous.' she wrote in her summary of the year.

Meanwhile, all hopes were pinned on *The Wombles* which was launched on 23 September 1968, at a lunch for the press and booksellers organised by Ernest Benn at Bouverie House, Fleet Street.

> I was briefed by John (Denton) and so to pre-lunch drinks. Met the artist Margaret Gordon, – nice, quiet, Bohemian, and the ladies and gentlemen of the press, E Benn directors, Osyth and reviewers. John made a speech about me and so did the chairman. Then up to lunch and I did my best to chat up booksellers. They all seem to think the book will go well – Benn's have printed 10,000 – my God, I hope it does or I shall have to run for it.

In a letter to me of 24 September to me, she wrote:

> We had a tremendous Wombles launching lunch yesterday … I was interviewed (which made a change, it's usually me doing it) and hope the blooming thing will sell. Harrods and Hatchards are going to push it and the Children's Book Centre. I kept looking at everybody swilling down their wine and chicken and trying to work out how many copies would have to sell to cover the cost of the spread!

Margaret Gordon's illustrations were charming but they were not the Wombles which were to emerge in a different form for the television series. Their first incarnation was a bear-like one: plump, spiky fur, round ears and a pointed nose. To be fair to the artist, even Liza did not know what they looked like! However, the illustrations and stories engaged the imaginations of children and those who read to them. The book did not fly off the shelves but sold solidly, enough to impress the children's book buyers at Hatchards and Foyles, who helped to maintain the orders momentum. American publishers Meredith, took up the option to publish in the United States in 1969 and Benns commissioned a second title, *The Wandering Wombles*, with Broadstairs once again giving Liza the respite and muse.

Gradually, over the course of 1969, the potential of *The Wombles* gathered momentum. The BBC began to show an interest in the books for their children's story-telling programme, *Jackanory*. It had begun in 1967 and the format was for a well-known actor to read a children's story to camera in a fifteen-minute slot from Monday to Friday. *The Wombles* was split into five sections – *Bungo, The Great Flood, The Snow Womble, Bungo's Great Adventure* and *The Midsummer's Party*. Ironically, although Bernard Cribbins proved to be the most popular *Jackanory* reader by far, he did not read the Womble stories. Ronald Hines, then a household name playing Wendy Craig's husband in the BBC series *Not in Front of the Children*, which ran for four series from 1967 to 1969 was chosen to read them. The first *Jackanory* Wombles were transmitted at the end of December 1969 and the beginning of January 1970.

A great shift was beginning to take place in Liza's life and if she had known what lay in front of her she would probably have run a mile. As it was, she was swept up by a Womble wave of such enormity that it threw her with a powerful ferocity onto the beach of fame and fortune.

Chapter 6

FilmFair and Fame

In December 1970 Max's BBC TV Outside Broadcast contract was not renewed and although he still retained his tennis radio commentary contract and *Going for a Song* on television, it was a crushing blow. His star was beginning to wane as Liza's took off. The BBC *Jackanory* series had shown the Wombles' potential to capture a television audience. At the same time, children's television characters were changing from two-dimensional cartoons or puppets with visible strings, to animated, stop-frame 3-D characters. *The Magic Roundabout*, first developed in France and then introduced to the British audience in 1966 with English scripts written by Eric Thompson, was animated by Ivor Wood, a hugely talented puppet maker and animator living in Paris. *The Magic Roundabout* had enormous success in the UK and continued to run until 1977 and it created a thirst for similar children's TV animations.

FilmFair, the American production and animation company founded by Gus Jekel in the United States in the 1950s, had set up a European office in the Rue de Belville, in the 20th Arrondissement in Paris, run by Graham Clutterbuck, a former advertising agency executive. Graham and Ivor Wood met and agreed to work together; it was a fruitful relationship which was to produce *The Herbs, Parsley the Lion, The Wombles* and *Paddington*. At first, Ivor commuted to London and then in 1969, the company relocated to Rathbone Place in London and subsequently to Jacobs Well Mews behind Baker Street in London. A second animator, Barry Leith, joined the team, fresh from creating an animation model of a Glow Worm heating boiler for a television advertisement. All the elements were in place for a Wombles lift-off.

FilmFair was just finishing a series of *Parsley* when John Denton at Ernest Benn sent a copy of *The Wombles* to Graham Clutterbuck to see whether he and Ivor thought there was any potential for animation. Graham recognised a winner when he saw one and took the idea to Cynthia Felgate, an executive producer of children's television at the

BBC. She was immediately interested but naturally wanted to see models, a pilot and costings. FilmFair was prepared to take a gamble and Liza was brought into the mix to write a pilot script. She sensed that Graham had doubts about her ability, 'Clutterbuck's worried about me. Will I be able to meet the script standard required? Oh dear,' she wrote in her diary on 1 April 1971.

Liza had a great deal of scripting experience under her belt in one way or another but stop-frame animation was quite a different kettle of fish. The pilot would be five minutes in duration with two frames per move and twelve moves per second for each character, moved manually. Liza was asked to write a story which would have one interior, one exterior and three characters in order to keep the costs down. At this point no one knew what Wombles really looked like. The Margaret Gordon spiky bear-like creatures? The *Jackanory* rather rat-like illustrations? Or the more recent Oliver Chadwick plump bears?

Ivor made the first prototype to resemble the Margaret Gordon illustrations in the original two books. Barry Leith recalls that:

The BBC felt that there were too many bears around and asked Ivor to think again. The next model had the beginning of a snout and big, floppy ears but the body was quite elongated and it had a tail. Cynthia Felgate thought this was too rodent-like so the third model had human-like paws which gave it 50 per cent more articulation potential, shorter legs and a plumper body. The black fur neck collar was to hide the articulation.

The final shape and look of the Wombles was born. Liza was thrilled. On 13 May 1971 she wrote to me at Manchester University:

One thing I should have liked you to see was the model (puppet) that Ivor Wood has made of a Womble. It's furry and has a long nose and the most beguiling expression. It also has twenty-five ball bearings which means that you can bend its joints in all directions. Any child would go mad over it and even the sober-minded businessmen at the meeting couldn't leave it alone so perhaps we may be onto a winner. Next week we have to present it to the BBC and I'm quite sure that it will sell itself.

She described Ivor as 'very gentle and very clever. A real artist.'

The sober-minded businessmen to whom she referred were John Hanson, who was Max's agent; Terry Flounders, a product merchandising expert; Brian Walsh, a solicitor; and Graham Clutterbuck. John, Terry, Brian, Max and Liza formed Wombles Ltd, to handle the patenting, licensing and promotion of the Wombles as and when the films were made and broadcast. Merchandising was in its infancy but *The Herbs* and *Parsley* had, according to Barry Leith, formed quite a little cottage industry. It was to be very different with the Wombles but they had a long road to travel before they got to the broadcast stage. They had considered starting the company before FilmFair's involvement when the *Jackanory* Wombles had been such a success and the book continued to sell well. Throughout 1970, Max and John Hanson had discussed its formation and by September John had brought in Terry. Liza wrote about them with some scepticism: 'Had drinks and then the dinner and then down to this hard business discussion. Oh men do talk a lot of hot air. On and on they went and all I decided was to ask for 51 per cent....'

The 'hot air' and difficult meetings were to become the bane of her working life until the company was dissolved in the 1980s. Liza always felt the cold wind of an overdraft just waiting to blow in, even when she was at the top of her earnings, and every cut of the percentage pie worried her. But she was a 'creative' and not 'a suit', so to her the endless meetings were anathema and a waste of time but she knew that they had to be endured. She hated confrontation in any form and many of the Wombles Ltd meetings would produce shouting matches. Max, although always looking out for Liza's best interests, was capable of stirring up trouble with his very stubborn, black-and-white approach to issues.

It took two years, 1971–73, and two pilots to get the Womble films onto television. The BBC had to be convinced. On Tuesday 2 February 1971 a Womble 'conference' was held at BBC Television Centre in White Hart Lane with Liza, Terry Flounders, Graham Clutterbuck and Monica Sims (Head of Children's Programmes) present. Liza was very pleased that Monica Sims was backing her: 'Monica Sims was exceedingly nice to me and deferred somewhat embarrassingly to me all the time! We broke up after five. The BBC want to run thirty five-minute Womble puppet programmes (starting) Autumn 1972 to replace *The Magic Roundabout*.'

The next step was to produce a pilot film. Liza set about writing the script, which was not an easy process and required some rewrites and breast-beating on her part. On 13 July she wrote:

Max and Marcus listening to the Test Match with shouts and groans. Up to the study to do another rewrite of the Womble script – not pleased with it – it's not right somehow and it's got to work bang off. Then we all changed and went to have dinner with Lionel Jeffries and family. What charmers they all are.

She finished the script finally on 15 July and the FilmFair team of Ivor and Barry finished building the set and the puppets and began filming. The sets were charming and intricate with all sorts of embellishments and jokes to delight viewers of all ages. The wallpaper was old copies of *The Times*, Great Uncle Bulgaria's daily newspaper found somewhere on the Common every day by young Wombles. An old car door served as a burrow door, heating pipes made out of old vacuum cleaners were strung along the wall. They were simply brilliant. The Womble puppets or models were manipulated to produce expressions – their snouts came in very useful for this – and they walked with the rocking motion of sailors on deck in a storm.

Liza went to see the first rushes at FilmFair on 6 October. 'Saw the Womble film – it was lovely. So funny and so endearing – you can't help liking them. They are creatures of great innocent charm. Ivor and Graham were very nice to me too which all helps.'

Then there was a deathly silence. On 13 October 1971, I heard from Liza: 'No Womble news yet. I feel in a totally euphoric state (but) shall feel like a lead balloon if we get the thumbs down. Everybody is after me at the moment: three publishers, DC Thompson, the BBC, COI! ... NOBODY is paying me anything.'

On the 25th there was an inkling of good news in Liza's next letter:

As to Wombles, I heard v. unofficially from the FilmFair boss's sec (Graham Clutterbuck's secretary) that <u>she'd</u> heard all the signs were good and would I hold myself in readiness, as they say, to be summoned to TV Centre with Ivor for a conference this Thursday or Friday since when I have heard nothing.

In her diary she took a more positive attitude:

> Call from Graham's secretary, who said could I go with Ivor to Monica Sims' meeting next week?
> 'Is that a good sign?'
> 'Yes.' Pause and then with a rush, 'Graham's in tremendous spirits – Monica loves it all except Jimmy Savile ... I've never seen Graham so optimistic.' I made a date, rang off and then yelled up and down the kitchen. Eventually rang Max. [he said] 'Don't be so certain. Now suppose *I* do the narration.'

Everyone who loved and loves *The Wombles* must be grateful to Monica Sims's dislike of Clutterbuck's first choice of narrator, Jimmy Savile. It is impossible to believe that the films would have had the same success had Savile done the narration. Worse still, the Wombles voices would have been associated with the most terrible crimes later revealed to have been perpetrated by Savile and the untold misery he caused. Instead, the wonderful Bernard Cribbins stepped into the world of the Wombles and brought his own brand of charm and brilliance.

Barry Leith remembers the search for the ideal narrator:

> Quite a few actors were tried out – Derek Guyler, Leslie Phillips, Bernard Breslaw – but when Bernard Cribbins came in to see us he decided to play the script with mutters, stutters and pauses. It was perfect. It gave the animators the chance to develop the characters between the words, with extra movements, glances and paw gestures.

Bernard Cribbins was a very talented and wide-ranging character actor and singer who was then at the height of his fame. He had recorded novelty songs such as *Hole in the Ground* (in the charts for thirteen weeks, reaching no 9) and *Right Said Fred* (no 10 in the charts) and was in many of the *Carry On* films. In the hugely successful film *The Railway Children*, released in 1970, he played Mr Perks, the loveable station porter and friend of the eponymous children. He brought all this experience to bear on his characterisation of *The Wombles*, including giving Madame Cholet a light and rather giddy French accent, inserting the odd 'ooh la la' into her dialogue.

I spoke to Bernard a year before he died and he remembered *The Wombles* with affection.

> I worked with Ivor in the studio and it was a lovely job, one of the most pleasant I had. The voices came from the way Liza had written them: Bulgaria was a general, Tobermory a Sergeant Major and Orinoco charming and lazy – it was all there in the writing.

With characteristic modesty, but somewhat incorrectly, he added, 'She was Shakespeare and I was doing a job.' Without Bernard's voice and characterisations the films would not have had the same level of success. The admiration was mutual, as Liza thought Bernard brought his own brand of magic to the animation. She loved Bernard's interpretations and from then on wrote his 'ums and ers' and accents into her scripts.

By mid-December Liza had written several scripts and another meeting with the BBC was convened, this time at FilmFair's office. Liza arrived in her Mini and John Hanson materialised, fed the parking meter, and took her to Durrants Hotel for a bracing tomato juice, where he told her he had got 'quite good terms' out of Graham Clutterbuck. Present at the meeting were Monica, Cynthia, Graham, Ivor and Barry, and it emerged that Graham had asked Ivor to rewrite one of the scripts. Ivor was furious with him, and Monica, the expert broadcaster, came down on Liza's side. It was true that Liza had no experience in writing this sort of script but it was her imagination and innate understanding of the Womble characters that were essential and unique. Josiane Wood, Ivor's widow, remembers accompanying Ivor to Wandsworth and 'thrashing out the stories round the dining table. Liza and Ivor adapted well to one another's strengths and while they worked out storylines I used to do the washing-up with Max!'

Barry Leith, the second animator, recalls:

> Elisabeth would knock up a few stories and we'd get them back and they'd only take forty-five seconds to read, but she freely admitted that she couldn't think of any more ideas. What we used to do, was

sit down and say the story needs a beginning, a middle and an end, a resolution. We'd take an item of rubbish that'd be nice for the model maker to make and then once we had that item we'd write a reason for why it was needed and then how it resolves itself in the end. We tended to think of rubbish that we could collect like cardboard and think what we needed that for and then we'd present that sort of scenario to Liza and say right 'fill that up with extra stuff'. She'd do her best on many occasions but sometimes she just couldn't do it. This was where Cribbins came in because he'd make it up and do a lot of his 'umming and arring' and he'd do a tapping of the foot and look at what we'd done to fill in the time.

This was not the last time that someone, in this case Graham Clutterbuck, who was not qualified as a writer, would mistakenly think that they could produce better scripts than Liza who had been writing for children for two decades and was, after all, the Wombles creator. Many years later this was to prove the downfall of other Womble reincarnations.

Once again, Monica Sims was helpful, as Liza recorded in her diary for 13 December:

Monica, once the dust had cleared, came down hard on my side and okayed my script and Cynthia was very nice to me – sees me as a willing pupil – well I AM! Ivor blew his top to me re-Graham – he really is overwhelmed and I know just how he feels. Well it's me out now, my bit is done, Monica having commissioned FilmFair to make the pilot of my script.

Filming began in January 1972 and by the end of the month Monica gave the unofficial green light which caused ensuing panic at FilmFair, with Ivor Wood ringing Liza and asking for more scripts urgently. 'As usual when there's a panic I did nothing except put tomorrow's dinner on to cook – THEN got down to it and belted out two scripts – bang, crash, wallop!'

The creation of the sets and filming were made under difficult operating conditions. The National Union of Mineworkers had called a strike in January which resulted in power rationing for a period in February, so Ivor and the team were working against the clock and the threat of power cuts. Then came a bombshell from the BBC. Ivor Wood rang Liza in the depths of despair:

> Monica didn't like the pilot film – everything had been halted. Ivor's puppets and my scripts were ok but she didn't like the animation, the background music, the narration etc etc. Ivor was obviously rock bottom. Felt my own stuffing drain away too … [drove] to FilmFair which was silent in the studio. Oh dear – Ivor! Had bought him a bottle to cheer him up – don't think it did. Barry [Leith] made coffee and we talked and talked and talked round and round the subject. Ivor brightened up a little.

Monica Sims decided to put in a BBC producer to oversee production but despite this setback there was a whiff of Womble potential in the air and the moneymen circled closer. Yet another Wombles meeting was held:

> I didn't understand 90 per cent of what they say re the company and the contracts, but how I bask, like some unlovely old shark in the respect of two (Terry and John) of my fellow directors – my wounded vanity smooths it on like oil. I haven't got a lovely character, I'm a megalomaniac probably, so have to make the most of it while it lasts. Quite by mistake (born out of desperation and whisky) it seems that something has been created which will make people fat, rich and revered so a bit of basking before they discover what a fraud I really am is satisfying.
>
> On 10 May Cynthia Felgate approved the pilot film (there was no sound at this point) and two weeks later Monica Sims gave her approval. Things were looking up. Liza wrote to me on 25 May, 'Monica Sims, Head of Children's TV BBC, has passed the Ws and wants a series, BUT the pilot film STILL has to be seen by Poorly [Paul] Fox [Head of BBC1] … However, there are kind of earth tremors going on and a general feeling of various people girding themselves up for settling final contracts as to who gets what … it's like that unnatural peace before the bang.

Finally, on 20 June: 'WOMBLES TAKEN BY BBC TV' she wrote in her diary, in joyous capital letters. The news came via Ivor as Liza was preparing a dinner party. She had taken a breather from chopping vegetables:

> Then, rather sagging about the ankles I answered the phone yet again. It was Ivor. He said that he'd got tired of waiting [to hear from the BBC] – his nerves stretched over the weekend – so he rang Cynthia Felgate who passed him on to the TV producer who is supposed to be overlooking things at FF and she said 'Oh haven't you heard?' Paul Fox had seen the film and was 'absolutely delighted' with it. So it was all on … I was lying on the dining room floor by now, in a kind of daze, nothing registering. It was sweet of Ivor to let me know. I finished off the dinner, rang Kate and told her, had a bath. Max in [from Queen's Club Championships] and grumbling dreadfully about everything.

The following day felt equally unsettled for Liza:

> I feel totally unreal. I just walked round and round and up and down … and round and round the garden. Talked to the trees, came in, had lunch but could not make myself concentrate on anything at all. In a very small way I think it's a kind of shock so went and lay down and dozed and dozed.

Later in the day, she and Max went to Simpsons for a tennis dinner and party. The pre-Wimbledon men's grass court championship at Queen's Club was underway. Some of the good and the great of the tennis world were on their table. Bea Walter (the former Wightman Cup Captain who had become a referee and who only two days later dismissed Pancho Gonzalez from the tournament causing a great furore) was 'in great form – spouting gossip – she's enormous fun'; Buzzer and Lois Haddingham (who became Chairman of the AELTC in the 1980s); the Barretts (commentator John and his wife, the tennis player Angela Mortimer); Virginia Wade (who was to win Wimbledon in 1977) 'who snubbed me bang into the ground', and a lot of the tennis press who were 'very nice'.

This was the perfect antidote to the Womble excitement and it was also diplomatically important to Max and Liza's marriage. Max was in *medias res* with the build-up to Wimbledon and always at his best at that time of the year, so although naturally very pleased about the Wombles' potential success, his *amour propre* remained intact and he was fully involved in his own exacting preparations. For the truth is that by 1972, the marriage was on rocky grounds and it was only the distractions of various events and the Womble developments which kept them together.

Through much of their married life Max had brief affairs and a long-time mistress. He was a handsome man with semi-celebrity status and very susceptible to flattery, so it was no surprise that women found him attractive. He was not at all clubbable with the exception of sport, especially cricket: he had kept wicket for the BBC 1st XI and played for the Lord's Taverners, the 'celebrity' club which raised money for good causes. But on the whole, he preferred the society of women who put him first. Liza, head down over her 'tryper' from dawn to dusk, fed him, did his laundry and made a substantial contribution to running costs which made him feel guilty on the one hand and neglected on the other.

Liza found Max's terrifying temper and increasing selfishness more and more difficult to deal with; she was no saint – she could never resist flirting – but she had remained faithful, until she had a shipboard affair in 1970 when she and Max were guest lecturers on the SS *Naivasha*. It was the most clichéd romance, a ship's officer who probably broke a woman's heart on every voyage, but it was a turning point for Liza who thereafter had fewer scruples about taking lovers and found great comfort in some very discreet, kind and loving men.

As the Womble television series was gestating, there was tremendous upheaval on Liza's domestic front. The greatest of these was in October 1971 – the purchase of a house in Spencer Park, a wonderful triangle of large, detached Victorian houses on the site of what was once Earl Spencer's land, facing onto Wandsworth Common. Later development had taken place on the eastern side, but it was only the original houses that had access to the 'secret garden'. At the end of each garden there was a small, private door which led onto several acres of semi-cultivated wilderness. There were avenues of trees, ancient rose-beds and a tennis court. Liza, who hated change, loved her new home. She became one of the volunteer gardeners, played tennis with neighbours and went on solitary circuits of the Park to plot books or just get away from the house and telephone. The house had belonged to James Fox, the actor, who had just forsworn acting for a life with the Christian Navigators.

He and Liza got along famously and she always held a soft spot for him thereafter.

Max wanted to retain the old house at No 4 Earlsfield and the adjacent house, No 2, which he had bought a few years earlier and converted into flat rentals. The idea was to convert No 4 into bedsits and for him to have an office there with his secretary – at this time the efficient, tolerant and great friend of the family, Annie Buckmaster – to oversee lettings and use it as a base from which to deal in Chinese blue-and-white porcelain. For several years, Charles Black, a very genial Jamaican, had been working for Max and Liza as a general handyman. By trade he was a carpenter but he was willing to turn his hand to anything and was a very reliable and much loved member of the Robertson household. The idea was that he would help with the conversions at No 4 and when possible give Liza a hand in the garden at Spencer Park.

This gave Liza a breathing space at Spencer Park: she was not short of work what with the FilmFair Wombles taking shape, a Wombles Annual to write, another magic novel and a new role at the COI as co-presenter of a news round-up with Ivor Mills, a former ITN anchorman, to name but a few commitments.

Following a recharging of her batteries in her beloved Alderney, Liza was back at her desk in September 1972 writing more Womble programme synopses – 'thinking of good ideas, they don't fall out of the air like ripe apples' – and she began *The Invisible Womble and Other Stories* for Benn and the indomitable Kaye Webb, who had commissioned the paperback for Puffin. Liza reckoned:

> It's not all that long – indeed it is very short – about 16,000 words only but each story has to be perfect in itself. Perfect indeed – what I mean is – start by catching your interest, pose a problem, make the problem worse and then come up with a tidy solution the clues to which must be laid from the start. All stories are, in a way, like detective stories. They incapsulate life and make it into a tidy and, I hope, entertaining shape.

Her creative peace was shattered when Max decided to sell the two Earlsfield houses, and in October they were sold to the Church of China and Max returned with Charles and Annie to base camp at Spencer

Park. Liza's office was what would have been a small bedroom, at the top of the stairs, overlooking the garden. Max requisitioned the morning room, a large, square office on the ground floor facing front towards Wandsworth Common and Trinity Road. In her summary of the year, Liza wrote:

> Funny really – it's meant the end of privacy for me – no more lovely solitude – the house is forever full of people but Max has shed himself of a responsibility which he had grown to loathe – made a lot of money and is now spending it as fast, if not faster, than he can go. I can't stop him … we gallop towards disaster, the sharks will have every penny off him but to try and stop the charge needs more courage and determination than I have.

The green light for the Wombles meant that Liza was turning out scripts, often based on Ivor and Barry's suggestions, as fast as she could while FilmFair made the programmes, frame by frame. The transmission date of February 1973 hung over their heads – and not just in the UK, the programmes had already been sold to Australia and New Zealand. In addition to the scripts, a TV annual was under discussion. She found the format inhibiting and became very self-conscious about it. 'Began that damned annual. I say damned because I'm scared of it never having written anything of the kind before. Am scared in other ways too as Hart-Davies are after me re the next magic book and supposing I CAN'T write?'

The Wombles were becoming all encompassing – not only the scripts and annual, but also Wombles Ltd business meetings to discuss possible licences, *The Wombles in Danger* – a Picture Puffin for Kaye Webb, and all the concomitant work such as giving talks at schools and libraries. Liza had a deep respect for librarians, and of a visit to the library at Elephant & Castle on 6 November she wrote:

> Such a pretty and beautifully dressed young librarian and a chap with long hair who had started work there this very day. They are dedicated – these young ones – they work hard for no great money and they are extremely nice in the best meaning of the word. Somebody should blow their celestial trumpets for them.

The following day she 'finished off the Cousin Yellowstone story for the annual, wrote two inspired synopses (I hope) and then two scripts'. On the 8th she gave a talk at a Walthamstow school ('good discipline') and on the 9th took part in what would now be called a brainstorming session, but she described as a 'think tank' with Wombles Ltd.

November 13th marked the 50th anniversary of the BBC and Liza felt she was definitely on her way up in the world when she was invited to a Radio Reception in the Council Chamber at Broadcasting House, even if her name was misspelt on the invitation as 'Miss Elizabeth Bereford'!

> It was great fun actually – all the current affairs lot were there but from *Woman's Hour* only Wynn Knowles – the Editor – so I was in most exalted company. John Timpson was there and came steaming over and stayed with me most of the evening … I felt very flattered … also met Wedgwood Benn and Vic Feather – so pretty high society. I kept wanting to say (to myself) 'why are you here? Go and do some work quickly.'

This lack of confidence in her ability was a running theme throughout Liza's writing life. At the end of November she met Kaye Webb and Dorothy Wood (Puffin) at FilmFair.

> We three ladies adjourned to the pub with our notes and it slowly became borne in old dimwit-me that THEY had never done a Picture Puffin like this before and were looking to me to tell THEM. After which it became much simpler as I can write a film script. It just goes to show that you should have confidence in yourself and I never EVER do. Cowardly to the end.

However, by the end of the year the Wombles phenomenon had already begun without a programme being shown. Although Liza had agreed to an outright fee of £50 an episode, a considerable raft of licences had already been agreed from soft toys to sleepwear which would bring in serious money and she was beginning to come to grips with what might lie ahead thanks to her creation.

> THEY have altered my life enormously because suddenly the pressure and the anxiety is off. I've had to work hard but it has brought in

sizeable money. Also, I like them. They haven't become ogres at all – there's something – some quality – which is basically so nice – that even a never ending tide of deadlines can't blight them. And even if disaster follows – what has been astonishing is the way that so many people – and a more varied crowd it's hard to find – have said to me 'I'm so glad that you're going to be successful.'... it pushes me back on my heels – it's so bloody generous of them. I'm sure I'd never be half as charitable!

There was just one more element missing from the films and that was the introductory and finale music. Barry Leith recalls that someone said there was a 'new kid on the block' called Mike Batt who did not have a great deal of experience. He was commissioned to write the music for the Wombles. Far wiser than Liza, however, Batt declined the £200 outright fee and asked for the character rights for musical production instead – the musical equivalent of public lending rights – which ensured that he got substantial royalties for years to come. Liza called him a 'modern Mozart' and they worked well together. 'I managed that rewrite of verses for Mike Batt and rang him. He was extremely nice about it. Sounds (at least) anxious to get everything <u>correct</u>.'

The jaunty *Underground, Overground, Wombling Free* title music became a national favourite and was to greet Liza and her family at every party they attended for years to come.

The new year began with gloom and doom. On 2 January 1973, Liza went to FilmFair where Ivor was feeling low. She wrote that 'Ivor was so depressing – everything on top of him – films no good – only going to run for twenty programmes – and he had piles of "P. Bear" [Paddington] books on his desk – so one can see which way the wind is howling – from the snows of Siberia.'

Inexorably, the pre-launch publicity began to shift up several gears, culminating in a day of interviews at the BBC. For once Liza was the interviewee, beginning with the *Today* programme and her old friend John Timpson:

So to the studio and did our piece – and it went very well although Robert Robinson muttered 'and so on that whimsical note we end.'

'Better whimsical than melancholic,' bristled Mrs R, and he actually laughed.

He and John are sweet-and-sour all right. I said thank you, and had a coffee in the canteen and then away to have my hair done and to see ghastly but probably truthful pics of self in the *Radio Times* – and so by taxi again to BH and Barbara Crowther [producer of BBC Radio's *Jack de Manio Precisely*] who was cross about me being on *Today*, and Jack who wasn't very friendly either. They seemed to think that I had tried to outsmart them which indeed I had NOT. Taxi to Global City (traffic awful) and by now I was starting to wilt – that dreadful neurotic-oh-God-I-must-have-10 mins peace sensation. Instead of which I had to make a speech and have my hideous photograph taken over and over again. Monica Sims, Vic Patrick [duty editor of *The Sunday Express* and Spencer Park next-door neighbour] and the press were there and John [Timpson] came with a whole *Today* team. I am no actress and was in a flat whirl. Had coffee with Wombles Ltd ... back home ... walked round the park and then off to *Nationwide* [BBC TV evening magazine programme] and a bloody girl who called Max Mr Beresford, God rot her.

The tactless BBC girl's faux pas was the moment when the fulcrum of success swung from Max to Liza and she recognised it. It was brought home to Max with sudden clarity that he was now the consort and she the queen. The following day he had what Liza described as a *crise de nerf*, when he broke down and cried 'all over the dining room' before leaving for an antiquing trip. There were only four days to go before the first transmission of *The Wombles*, but instead of a build-up to fame and fortune there followed an almost farcical let-down in the manner of an Ayckbourn play. Liza developed a sore throat and lost her voice and became thoroughly fed up and depressed as she was forced to give up smoking (temporarily) and then on Monday, 5 February, transmission day.

'What should have been a five-star day was dreadful. Trissie was by then 92 and living in a residential nursing home. Sister Anne rang to say Ma being taken into hospital,' Liza wrote in her diary. She drove to the Balham nursing home where she found her mother in a dreadful state and in pain.

Followed two very nice ambulance men to St James Hospital where HELL began because nobody wanted to know – they were an urgent accident hospital only, St Johns dealt with geriatrics but Ma was not in their 'catchment area'. I smiled and buttered up and tried somewhere, somehow, to find someone who would take responsibility and all the time she was in pain and bewildered. It was horrible. At one point I chased the Admissions Officer right into the men's loo!

She succeeded, and with Trissie ensconced in Ward 20 she raced home to watch the first programme and then charged off with Max to Soho and dinner with the FilmFair crew, 'a bonus at the end of the day'. The next morning the phone was red hot with congratulations and telegrams and cards were delivered – but … 'This should be the greatest period of my life instead of which I feel ill, tired and deeply depressed but mustn't let on.'

Trissie recovered but Liza's life had changed forever.

Chapter 7

Womble Mania

When the first series of *The Wombles* ended on 2 March 1973 after fifteen episodes, they had become firm family favourites. The programmes were transmitted at 5.40 pm, followed by the BBC News at 5.45, so they were seen by adults as well as children and the humour and charm appealed to both age groups. One unintended consequence of this new-found fervour for the Wombles was that the number of visitors to Wimbledon Common shot up and children left litter to try and tempt Wombles into broad daylight. The Rangers were less than amused. It was not just children who believed in the Wombles' existence. Within four days of the first programme's transmission, there were headlines in the *London Evening Standard* and *Evening News* that the Wombles were putting the Rangers out of work because they were doing their job for them!

The pace did not slacken for Liza, quite the opposite. She was still – as she disparagingly called it – 'banging out' scripts for FilmFair where Ivor and Barry were making the next fifteen episodes due for transmission in June; three Womble picture books for Benn; the first *Wombles Annual* for World Distributors; the synopsis for yet another romantic novel, *Saturday's Child;* and her sixth magic book, *Invisible Magic.* The magic book was an idea too many with which to cope. Throughout July she suffered from writer's block – 'My mainspring seems to to have gone. Why isn't there an author's plumber?'.

And Liza was still interviewing for *Woman's Hour.* Over the years she had lugged the cumbersome reel-to-reel recorders to every imaginable location and interviewed the humble to the hallowed. Celebrities in those days were either stars or achievers. There were three television stations – BBC1 and 2, and ITV – BBC Radio and the new commercial local radio stations such as LBC and Capital Radio only began in 1973, so BBC radio interviews were of huge interest to audiences who wanted to know more about their favourite actors, writers, movers and shakers. On the whole Liza found actors a dream to interview:

One of the many lovely things about actors is that you don't have to bother. Give them a cue, put your chin in your hands, nod, listen, exclaim and you can tot up the week's bills, write the opening para of a script and decide how to parcel out tomorrow's chores while they tell you about their last part.

Among those she interviewed in 1973 were fellow children's authors. Kathleen Hale (*Orlando the Marmalade Cat*), who was 'small in height, stout in figure, white short hair with fringe, somewhat abrupt manner, charming voice and must have been most attractive when young. She did a very good interview. How she hated Enid Blyton.' Raymond Briggs, whom she found 'shy and has a rough, dry skin and high colour and is also having a great success with his book *Father Christmas*. Drew an interview out of him.' A third writer was Richard Adams, the civil servant who had caused a storm with *Watership Down*, the charming story of a colony of rabbits whose warren was threatened by development. She felt bewitched by his blue eyes but found him 'a difficult man, the scratchy thorn about to emerge as a blooming rose. Gave a good interview.'

On 17 April, Liza reflected on the past few months with increasing bitterness:

The Wombles were a success – it was a strange situation in which all kinds of people turned up trumps and gave me a great deal of help and support AND publicity. John Timpson in particular stood by me, and the national press – so I was here, there and everywhere and yet I was utterly depressed. That awful, black, humiliating affair with Ma being ill and the hospital not wanting to take her – the total disinterest, even cruelty of the staff. I've been a journalist for thirty years and been in some pretty rough situations but never had I met such total callousness, dislike and bitterness. It appalled, saddened, struck at me and for all that month which should have been so marvellous, I felt old, sick, shrivelled and unhappy. I've always loathed February but this time it as even worse – like crawling though some sickening, smelly tunnel, and yet the Wombles did win through. The letters came thick and fast – success – and suddenly it was bandwagon time. And on they all got with their cement-filled boots: the management, then the PROs, the wheelers and dealers – they use us – the Ivors, Barrys, and me's of this world – but we despise them. Without us they wouldn't exist, without them we still work. I have had the great success for which I've worked for thirty years and does it bring gaiety? Warmth? A sensation of being carefree, in its wake? Does it hell, I could cut my bleeding throat.

Depression, never clinically diagnosed, was something which Liza suffered from throughout her adult life. It seemed to take her in its murky grip after periods of intense work and writing activity. The family was unaware just how much this affected her – she would talk about life's elastic 'going twang' – and there is little doubt that Max's increasingly strange behaviour and profligacy unsettled her considerably. The trauma of her father leaving home and her mother's anguish would revisit her. She wrote constantly about not being 'worthy' and 'it's all my fault', the accusations Trissie made in her childhood bubbling to the surface.

She visited Alderney in April and the island worked its usual soothing balm of the soul.

[*The Wombles*] has turned out to be a quite extraordinary success. Now I know it because the island children seem to have drawn me into a secret society of under 12s. Everywhere I go they come towards me and tell me all the plots. In shops, in the street, in gardens, back kitchens. I love it, love it because they're interested, because its talking directly to people with absolutely no 'keep clear' signs in between. It's the direct interchange of ideas where imagination, thought-question-solution slip and fuse – explode – and throw up more ideas, laughter, interest, questions. There is a sort of pure incisiveness which does illuminate the landscape – we're all giving and receiving equally. It's an unbelievable, extraordinary feeling when some unknown, un-named child comes up to you and begins to explain exactly what the Wombles are all about.

At the end of 1973 she summed up her feelings about the Wombles on television:

It all started so uncertainly. We hoped, we trusted, but we didn't know what would happen. It was a good idea, the films had charm

… but they are after all, only five-minute puppet films but somehow, by some strange alchemy, they appealed to people from babies to old age. Everybody seemed to find in them something which they liked – understood – felt familiar with and (to me) perhaps most important of all, the Wombles made them LAUGH. Over and over again all sorts and kinds of people have told me what the Ws mean to them. In eleven months they have become (however fleetingly one doesn't know) part of folklore. Everybody it seems from the businessman to the dropout 6-yr-old knows about them and translates them to their own lives! … What I wanted to do was to create a society and a background with a way of life which, in a shifting, changing world, would epitomise security – of knowing who you were and where and knowing too that if you stepped outside that way of life you would be punished – accept the punishment and that would be THAT. I wanted to give to children 'Four walls, a roof, a family, friends, work and FUN'. And it worked, God, it worked. In a tiny, trivial, minute way, *The Wombles* made a lot of people happy … There is something about them, their personalities, a basic 'niceness' that has defied and made nonsense of greed, stupidity, cupidity. I have never for a second been sorry that they were created or regretted them. I like them as much now as I ever did, and still feel that with a Womble for a friend you are safe. I think that in them, somehow, is the best that was in Father R and Aden and Mother, Max, Marcus, me, Kate.

There, I believe, is the crux, the very ethos of the Wombles: Liza's desire for security and fun. Goodness knows what a psychiatrist would make of it, but her precarious childhood and uncertain adulthood produced the furry inhabitants of Wimbledon Common who spent their time having fun while restoring order.

The Wombles may have been 'safe friends' for children, but they were turning into a burgeoning industry for those involved with them. Mike Batt felt inspired to follow his success with the programme title song, *Underground, Overground*, with an album of Wombling Songs and very soon formed a band of musicians. On 27 July, Liza had Mike and his wife over to dinner and he played the songs on the old upright piano in Marcus's bedroom. 'Like 'em very much. He is extremely clever,' Liza noted in her diary. The LP was issued in November of 1973 and spent seventeen weeks in the UK album charts, reaching number nineteen in March 1974. In January 1974, he appeared on the *Cilla Black Show* wearing a Womble costume (Orinoco) that his mother had made for him to plug *The Wombling Song*. Consequently, when the single got into the charts, the band was asked to perform on *Top of the Pops*. The Wombles pop and rock group was officially born and Womble costumes were made for the other band members. Batt followed this success with a further four Womble albums which all 'went gold'.

Before the band formed, however, the television series – the second fifteen programmes were shown in June 1973 – had propelled Liza onto a new level. Her book sales were increasing – 'apparently Wombles have been top of the bestseller list for the last two weeks' she wrote on 17 May – and licensing revenue prospects were so good that Max was talking about going to live in Alderney to avoid the prohibitive highest rate of taxation in the UK which was then 80 per cent, plus a further tax on unearned income. Liza knew he would 'go mad' there and so the subject was dropped, but only temporarily.

By August, FilmFair was in discussions with the BBC about a second series: 'Ivor says Monica Sims wanted another thirty programmes for 1975. Shall I be asked to write them?' The answer was yes and her outright fee was increased to a majestic £75 per programme, a 50 per cent increase. Her fame was increasing as well. After a visit to Arding & Hobbs, the local department store at Clapham Junction, she wrote tongue-in-cheek in her diary:

> We were welcomed royally by the supervisor who said all the Womble slippers had sold out. Head Office wanted to send me a present, the Manager wanted to meet me etc etc and then got almost the same treatment in Boots! … Walking up Battersea Rise I heard three small boys one saying 'I've got Orinoco!' And that's IT – fame!

By the end of the year Germany, Denmark and Japan had expressed interest in publishing the Womble books and *De Wombels* had appeared on Dutch television. The UK was working a three-day week because of the power shortages and as Liza worked her way towards Christmas she was feeling the strain. 'Got to Sainsbury's at 10.30 – IT WAS HELL,' she wrote with exasperation. 'People are spending like it's the end of the world – and a lot of the power isn't working – so you go into this half-lit supermarket where half the goods aren't on the shelves anyway.'

On Christmas Eve at St Anne's church, the first half of the service 'was lovely with candlelight flickering and processing carols. For a moment the true religious life was there but then my trousers fell down and I had to take communion holding them up!' Determined to see the funny side she wrote, 'I think Jesus would smile.'

At the end of the year she wrote:

What a bloodstained year! A year of freedom in a way – from financial anxieties of the old sort. For the very first time EVER in my life that pinch was off. I became, in a small way, rich. And discovered that I didn't know what to do with money. If you're the kind of person who goes on saving up bread crumbs and baking them (when the oven is on anyway) you're THAT sort of person. It seems sinful to spend it on clothes or cosmetics or even taxis. You are imprisoned by forty-seven years of being scared about paying bills.

1974 was, if anything, even busier for Liza. The bandwagon was overcrowded with agents, advertisers and artistes all wanting a slice of the Womble pie. A Womble musical was to be produced by Bill Kenwright with music by Mike Batt and script by Liza; a large range of merchandising was 'coming in thick and fast', which eventually included stuffed toys, bedroom slippers, stationery, stickers, figurines, bath soap, night lights, lamp shades, chocolate bars, gelatine pudding kits, posters, games, shirts, badges (buttons), cloth patches, and nightwear.

As a result of this, Liza was in greater demand than ever. On 11 March for example, she and Barry Leith were driven up to Birmingham in the BBC minibus with two sets and three Wombles, to be interviewed on *Pebble Mill at One*, the BBC magazine programme which was then the flagship of new 'daytime' television. They were on with an eclectic guest list.

I met John (Lord) Oaksey who was very nice; an ex-convict who had the most alive eyes I've ever seen; and George Hamilton IV who was SPLENDID. 'I surely do like your Wombles, E-lis-a-beth' – I nearly fainted! My piece seemed to go ok and then there was a reception afterwards – everybody loved the Ws, the lighting men, cameramen, all of them. It's quite extraordinary.

The next day, she gave Bernard Cribbins a scrambled egg lunch to discuss scripts and then drove with Annie Buckmaster to Stoke Park, Guildford, to present prizes at the Agricultural Show.

We had to wait for 'Bungo' who came on a later train as he was mobbed at Waterloo! The chairman of the Agricultural Committee, an elderly and most respected man, got quite annoyed when I tried to tell him the Wombles <u>didn't</u> exist before I invented them. It wasn't a leg-pull either, most extraordinary.

On 20 March, she and Mike Batt did a 'royal' tour of the Ideal Home Exhibition and a few days later she was off to Hackney to lecture, driven by son Marcus who was home from Haileybury for the Easter holidays.

I felt really rough, think I had a temperature last night so MCR, God bless him, volunteered to drive me, thank goodness … Arrived at the church half an hour late but the vicar was lovely and kind and had been leading community singing, and the Borough Librarian (probably the most boring man in the WHOLE WORLD) had played the organ and <u>loved</u> it! There were about 300 kids, and I talked away with fast flashes when the world seemed to be receding and thought 'Oh God, I'm going to faint and I MUSTN'T', and I didn't either. And then they mobbed, pouring over me, was worried a small one might get knocked over and trampled but it was OK … Went to look at the library (that's what I call 'The Royal' bit) and then on to an extraordinarily dull lunch … on to the next library and a nice, quiet restrained talk.

By mid-April her batteries were beginning to run down. She had done *Start the Week* on Radio 4: 'They were all so clever – Jonathan Miller, Edward de Bono, Harriet Crawley, Robert Robinson, and when they began to talk about lateral thinking Bernard Cribbins and I didn't know what the hell they meant. We clung together and hoped we put on a fair show'. Then she went on to a book signing at Hamleys:

Spent the day autographing books and talking to children. They were great, I can listen and talk to them all night AND the parents … people say all kinds of things and it's marvellous because the Wombles do seem to have been fun and laughter for all kinds and sorts of people. They came from Belfast, Scotland, China (!), America and S. America and they LIKE the Wombles and they tell me about THEM and it makes them smile.

Finally, she had thrown an impromptu party at which Kaye Webb pleaded 'Oh Liza don't send me home to that musty house,' so Liza made up a bed for her while the future Chief Justice of Kenya was falling about downstairs; 'it was a smash hit party,' Liza observed. The next morning Mike Batt, Wendy, and their daughter arrived to go through the lyrics and music of his second Womble album. 'Mike upstairs to play the latest music on the cracked old piano while he bellowed out the lyrics. I kept him firmly upstairs until he'd gone through everything. He is ENORMOUSLY talented.'

That same day her cousins came to lunch and she went to a dinner party at near neighbours. The 'elastic' was beginning to go and the next day she was off to Alderney, escaping from the exigencies of her new fame. Naturally enough, reaction soon set in and her spirits plummeted to the depths, so much so that at one point she briefly considered suicide, I suspect as a result of too much to drink as well as exhaustion and marital problems.

For the next eighteen months the pressures never really let up. The stage shows were underfunded, under-rehearsed and not thought through properly. *The Wombles* musical was launched simultaneously in nine theatres across the UK in December 1974 and closed within a few weeks on 18 January 1975 – not even Mike's music could rescue them. *The Wombles* stage characters were panned for being too thin, inaudible, and in one theatre the backstage was so visible that children were traumatised when they saw a Womble take off its head. Liza went to the opening at the Shaftesbury Theatre in London on 16 December.

It was, if not a disaster, just awful. One-third full and children shifting and talking all the way through and me trying to be cheerful. Max was very good – he did try like anything to chat people up – and MCR too – but it was death and disaster. Actors tried hard but it was tatty. Bad scenery, bad sound, bad lighting etc etc. It makes you squirm and it's bad over all from a Womble point of view. I went up to the dressing rooms to talk to them and try and put in a little life and gave them some bottles of wine. But it's no good, it's woefully bad and it should have been marvellous. Came home sadly defeated … it's all my fault … I should have taken more time and trouble.

However, Mike Batt had released his second Womble LP and the Wombles band appeared on *Top of the Pops*, which helped to keep the public awareness up. The second series was transmitted in 1975, starting on 15 September, which blotted out the uncomfortable memories of the musical debacle.

In February 1975 Liza spent some time in her house in Alderney and noted:

My life has changed convulsively in the last year. In January I felt totally overloaded with responsibility which is why I ran away [to Alderney] but in this little house I'm only me – not famous – not responsible to THEM – only responsible for cleaning and tidying and cooking. The friendly tick of the fridge, the roar of the boiler, the occasional voices outside … they are balm and tranquillity.

In a way, she did escape again when she and Max went on a two-month tour of South Africa. He had acquired some commentary work there and at the last moment, Liza decided to go with him.

The SS *Windsor Castle* sailed from Southampton on 14 March, but not before Liza and a costumed 'Great Uncle Bulgaria' had been filmed and interviewed by the press. 'GUB was great but extremely nervous … goodness it was cold!'.

Once they had set sail, Liza auditioned various staff to play the role of GUB when required at lectures on board. A 'purserette' called Michelle got the part, 'and Roger the very superior young purser did not and <u>sulked!</u>' Although by her own admission she was not a good sailor, she seemed to have survived the voyage remarkably well and gave lectures in the ship's cinema about her life with the Wombles. One of her cribs survives, written in a shaky hand due to the motion of the ship. It includes:

Apologise for not being short, fat and furry
How it started
Book
Second Book – Prince Edward (reputedly a fan)
TV series – BBC rules. Writing the scripts, opening credits, bottles
Making the puppets – the way they work – 8 days = 5 mins
Making the sets – puppet limitations
Telephone system at Cannizaro Park, nude on ceiling
Bernard Cribbins – dubbing
Music – Mike Batt, go through lyrics, translations at midnight.
Do Wombles lay eggs?
Rules in public, drunk in Glasgow, DOG
Womble at Waterloo
Highly gifted children
Letters
Licences 140+ – everything has to be vetted

The phone system at Cannizaro House, an eighteenth-century house (now a hotel) which stands on the edge of Wimbledon Common, may have had a pre-STD switchboard in the early Seventies and may have captured Liza's imagination. However, the 'phone system' in the Womble Burrow was more nautical with a 'blow-and-speak' system. As to the nude on the ceiling, I can only surmise that it was the cue for a funny story of which she always had plenty.

At first Liza found it very dull on board and thought everyone 'very old', but within a week she was enjoying life aboard the little ship immensely.

My early mornings are very busy! At 8, I stagger to the gym and go through this very funny routine. Dick and Violet [fellow travellers] pace by … so do Helen and Jim and then when I'm in a muck sweat and the masseuse has stopped masseuring [*sic*] that large lady with the discontented face … then I stagger awf [*sic*] again, quite purple by now, to flop into the pool while 'The Battle of the River Plate' pounds about putting his lido deck in order. Down for breakfast (two

Ryvitas) and into the Lounge for dancing by 9.45! No wonder that I flop on deck after all THAT! Have no lunch, more swimming, more sun bathing, more sleeping … Then the BBQ which was terrific, danced with the Commodore.

On Thursday, 27 March, they docked at Cape Town and she felt sad to leave 'that cosy, luxurious womb'. Almost before her feet landed on terra firma, she was commandeered for interviews with *Die Burger,* an Afrikaans daily newspaper and *Afrikaans Radio.* From then on she and Max enjoyed socialising, sight-seeing, promoting the Wombles and, in Max's case, preparing for the South African Open Tennis Championship. All went smoothly until the day they left Cape Town, Thursday 3 April.

Goodbye beautiful Cape Town … Max was fussing a bit about the car and at one time got the overdrive locked so that he couldn't STOP. Got it right again. Up into the mountains and a lorry pulled left ahead of us – and slowed – it swung across us. I yelled 'Max, he's turning right!' and WMR just didn't seem to react. He says he accelerated. Anyway we hit it … a dreadful crunch – the windscreen went, we hit a boulder and then in what seemed like slow motion we turned over twice. We were strapped in but I hit the the car roof with my left shoulder. There was a silence – we got out – I lay on the wing – a man appeared against the sky, 'I'm a doctor, can I help?' Oh the luck, everybody was so kind. I was driven to a small, quiet hotel and put to bed. People came in whispers. Dr Jim Lane, wife (NZ) winsome, four beautiful children all stayed with us.

They were lucky. Max was unscathed and Liza got away with whiplash and inflamed muscles, so they were able to carry on to Johannesburg where there was tennis commentary for Max at Ellis Park, while Liza continued on her round of merchandising meetings, book signings and interviews, with Great Uncle Bulgaria in tow. One evening at a barbecue, she met the American actor Charlton Heston who was in South Africa promoting *The Four Musketeers: Milady's Revenge,* in which he played Cardinal Richelieu. She found him, 'large and nice and a bit older than one expected'. As they were having their photograph taken together he advised her to hold her chin up as it looked better in photos; certainly his chin was always prominent!

At this time South Africa still did not have television, much to the frustration of most of the country. While Max and Liza were there, the nascent South African Broadcasting Company was testing programmes for transmission, based in Johannesburg. While at the Rand Agricultural Show, Liza watched one of these programmes on the company's show stands. 'Watched their first transmission which was ok.'

On 29 April, following a couple of days in a game reserve, the Robertsons left South Africa and flew home in a Jumbo jet – 'like six London double-deckers – I hated it'.

Back home once more, Liza was more relaxed than she had been for some time. While in South Africa she had been feted, fed and watered without having to cook a single meal, write nothing other than letters and probably best of all, no Wombles Ltd board meetings. In 1975, at the height of licensing demand, the board meetings had become almost toxic. The businessmen wanted the income, Liza and Max were determined not to sully the Womble brand with slipshod goods or association with non-Womble products such as alcohol. She debated the issue with Tim Benn, Director of Ernest Benn:

> There is a point when you really don't know what is right or wrong – black, grey, white. Tim says passionately that the children of America living in a mucky country need the Wombles because (hopefully!) they'll make the children happier, tidier, more aware of conservation etc. But in order to fulfil that 'need', does it mean that I have to agree to the sponsorship of General Foods and have no right of veto of what commercials are used in ad breaks? I did say strongly that I would not have the Wombles used IN a commercial … I only want to protect children from the pressures of buy, buy, buy. It seems such a basic truth but it vanishes very quickly.

It was a full-time job trying to protect the Womble ethic, especially once 'pirate' brands started to appear, manufactured in the Far East usually, and without permission or payment.

The demand for the written word also increased beyond Liza's capacity. In addition to the novels and picture books, there were gift books, annuals, comic strips, syndicated columns, even diaries. I was drafted in to help write contributions to the annuals and Collins diaries for children, and a local journalist, John Passmore, was authorised to write a regular Womble column for *The Wimbledon News*.

There were award ceremonies to attend as well. The Eleanor Farjeon Award (Liza never won) recognising significant contribution to children's fiction, that year was held at the Biba Roof Garden in Kensington.

> I stared bemused and rather depressed at all the writers of children's books. They were so OLD and grey and dull and all being nasty about each other. It was depressing. I sat outside during the speeches which went on and on. Naomi Lewis's (recipient of the award) long, long talk was somehow a sad reflection of loneliness. I felt the grey, chill winds of depression.

The winds were dispersed by a chance encounter. Marcus had accompanied Liza and Max to the awards and, now aged 19, his eye had alighted on a pretty girl called Julia. Much to his amazement, she introduced herself as his stepsister; when her mother came to talk to her, Julia introduced Marcus to his stepmother, whom he had never met. The woman was Max's first wife Nancy Suttor, and Julia was her daughter from her second marriage. Nancy was now in publishing and was an award invitee. Marcus recalls:

> Mum then came up to us so I introduced her to Dad's first wife and then eventually Dad came up and said in typical brusque fashion, 'Come on, it's time to go'. Nancy looked at him and said 'Don't you recognise me, Max?' and he said, 'No, should I?' and so I then introduced my father to his ex-wife!

Liza reported that there was a total lack of charm all round but she did find the situation very funny in retrospect and she and Marcus often retold the story.

1975 proved to be a landmark year in Liza's life. On 11 October Trissie died, aged 95. It was something that Liza dreaded and welcomed in equal part: welcomed because Trissie's health had been declining and she had become increasingly depressed. The nurse at her home – Sister Anne –

had an incurable brain tumour and they were good friends. Anne died during the night and it was subsequently discovered that same morning that Trissie was having a heart attack and she was admitted to the Bolingbroke Hospital, Wandsworth Common. When Liza saw her she was shouting and bewildered (but never senile).

I asked the young doctor what he thought of her chances and he more or less said 50/50. Made it quite plain to him that I thought it was pointless to try to save her. He said it was against his ethical code, but I take the full responsibility. She knew nothing of what had happened to Anne but what lay ahead for mother without her? I held on to mother's hand – her right – and repeated the *Ave Maria* over and over again. I went home and waited … I rang the hospital at 6 pm and was ok then. About 6.45 they called me and asked me to come. Kate went with me. Ma was dead when we arrived. The doctor told us she had sat up and asked for a cup of tea, sat back and died. Kate and I went to see her – she was still warm and very elegant and fierce and noble, like a dead empress. I kissed her goodbye and asked her to give my love to Dad.

At the end of the year, Liza was able to reflect on Trissie's life more dispassionately:

During the last few weeks [of her life] she had grown very depressed. Over and over again she said it was unlike anything she had ever felt before. I wonder if – at last – she felt that wonderful energy and her remarkable body were starting to fail, that she sensed it at the back of her mind but refused consciously to accept it. That she was aware of the approach of death … that to BE was really all that counted, that to be dead was lost and forgotten forever. She was a great force – character, emotion, body, but childlike, she had never grown in any other way. I am not decrying her, indeed I have the utmost admiration for her tremendous strength. She took hold of life and shook it until its bones rattled. She lived life as few people do … there was never anything wishy-washy about her. Maybe one day I can do her justice in a book, someone should. Strong people <u>are</u> frightening and we hide behind them, use them as scapegoats and as excuses for our own light weight ... In a way she gave me the long incubation period which has resulted in the astonishing Womble success. Like most writers, I was writing out all that had been kept battened down inside. I _am_ glad that at least she was aware of that success because fame, prestige, glory, were the breath of her life. She adored importance and recognition and, even if in a childish, weird way, she has got that all over the world as Madame Cholet.

Chapter 8

The Alderney Burrow

Liza increasingly found that Spencer Park was the antidote to the rough and tumble of business deals, the pressure of Womble promotion and the antagonistic boardroom scenes, and an escape from her worries in general. She was at her happiest when out in the garden with a spade and secateurs, digging and planting her vegetable garden or snipping back shrubs and roses in the private park. All her life she was an escapist – from confrontation, from decision-making, from people, from reality. Alderney was her beloved bolt-hole from London and responsibilities, but Spencer Park was on her doorstep. There were interesting people living around the Park; there were those who had lived there for decades, and who watched with slight incredulity and bewilderment as the houses were sold to 'showbusiness people'; there were actors and theatre directors, lawyers and even a Concorde pilot. The second group mystified the first, but Liza bridged the two worlds successfully. The second group held glamorous parties, as did Liza and Max, whereas the first group invited one to tea. This fascinating mini-soap opera was vastly entertaining and the park itself provided a wonderful setting in which the action took place. Liza's imagination was fired by the park, too. Its mystery was magical and became a backdrop for several of her magic books.

Why, then, did she contemplate leaving it? The answer is she didn't want to leave at all, not even to go and live in Alderney, which was her retreat from Max and Womble pressures. It was Max who was determined to beat the taxman and leave the UK while taxation was still outrageously high and Liza said firmly that the only tax haven she would move to was Alderney. He was not alone in his thinking: professionals were leaving the country (the 'brain drain') and whole businesses were relocating. Unfortunately, but rather typically, the Robertson timing was to prove wrong.

By the end of 1976 it was apparent that the Wombles' popularity had peaked. New stop-frame characters arrived on the block such as *Ivor the*

Engine and, more importantly, *Paddington Bear.* The latter was animated by Ivor Wood at FilmFair and was to become a firm favourite in the national consciousness. This was not to say that the Wombles disappeared from the BBC schedules: the original sixty programmes from the two series were repeated many times, sometimes at the earlier hour of 09.35. Mike Batt turned his attention to new projects too, and did not record any more Womble LPs after 1976 until several decades later. However, there was still demand for books and annuals: four picture books for Ernest Benn – *The MacWomble's Pipe Band, Madame Cholet's Picnic Party, Bungo Knows Best* and *Tobermory's Big Surprise,* plus the penultimate Wombles novel, *The Wombles Go Round the World,* and an annual for World Distributors *The World of the Wombles.*

Liza recognised what was happening and wrote in her year-end diary summary: '*The Wombles* popularity has decreased. Fan mail has gone down and so have merchandising sales and therefore revenue.'

In August she passed the landmark birthday of 50 and wondered whether her writing skills were still up to par. She had turned her thoughts to writing adult fiction but she knew not what, other than romantic. She wanted to be like her father and write books that would stand the test of time. Her brother Marcus – now calling himself Marc Brandel – had written several novels, including *Survivor,* published that year which had good reviews and is still in print today. He was living partly in Ireland and partly the USA, from where he wrote to Liza to thank her for her congratulatory letter.

> It was kind of you to write, and I'm glad you enjoyed *Survivor.* I suppose it's what is known as a fairly 'good read'. The trouble is I can't write books like that quickly enough! …I'm in Northern California, doing some research on another book – I've already been fussing around with it too much. Then I'm going down to Los Angeles looking for a television assignment.

Marc must have seemed very sophisticated in his writing and lifestyle to Liza. I remember him as a very good-looking and rather exotic uncle who drifted in out of our lives very, very occasionally. He was supportive of Liza but she never quite believed that her writing was as good as his. Her eldest brother, Tristram, also used to descend from his Olympian heights and bestow advice and instruction with the patronage of a bishop and a faint astonishment that Liza had made a successful writing career for herself. It really was not a surprise that she had a faint inferiority complex and longed to achieve something with 'proper' writing.

Liza was no longer working for *Woman's Hour*, rather she was touring endless bookshops and libraries giving talks with the occasional book promotion or Womble event. A very special visit, the memory of which she cherished, was to the aircraft carrier *Ark Royal* on 18 November 1977. The crew had adopted the Wombles as a mascot and invited Liza and Great Uncle Bulgaria to come aboard at Plymouth.

Marvellous view of Plymouth Hoe from my hotel. Picked up by Lt-Commander Potter – both of us in a highly nervous state – and driven to Ark Royal. I hadn't thought what an RN ship would be like … was welcomed aboard and in full evening rig I had to climb a ladder, clamber over pipes and gear to the Captain's cabin. Captain Anson was a tough, craggy (nervous) man and we were making conversation when GUB (John Tucker) arrived. He stood in the doorway, held out both arms to me and said 'MOTHER!' The captain, half in, half out of his chair was a picture. GUB and I embraced both trembling with nerves. Along to the hangar where about 500 of the ship's company had assembled – so young but so like the sailors I remember. The Band of HMS *Ark Royal* then struck up 'Overground, underground' [*sic*], GUB made his entrance and the sailors went mad. The BBC recorded a bit then I was introduced up onto the platform and got a standing ovation. Made a very short speech and all laughed in the right places and then more ovation as I presented Orinoco (fur toy) to the captain … They sang at the tops of their voices – it was a stunning moment in my life. I talked to quite a lot of the men and took their photographs and all the time the marine band was playing magnificently and for a little while I saw those other sailors, the ones I knew (in the war) who shaved with rationed razor blades, had hard soap, little hot water, stiff, uncomfortable uniforms who were always tired and scared and rather underfed; whose hair styling was short-back-and-sides. They were rough and tough, dusty, knocked about, bewildered and young. For me, they were there and I saw them. They were different and the same. And that was marvellous because you see the jaunty way of standing, the feeling of belonging, the laughter and the shouting at officers.

The Crew and Band of HMS *Ark Royal*, conducted by W/O Sheppard, released a recording (45rpm) in January 1977 of *The Wombling Song* and *Remember You're A Womble*, which can be found on YouTube. Listen to that and you get some idea of what Liza heard that evening: magic.

Finally the decision was made to up sticks and live in Alderney and had they gone in 1977 there might have been significant savings, but in true Max fashion he considered 22 Little Street a basic holiday home which needed a total overhaul before moving in. And in true Alderney fashion, this took nearly two years to achieve!

Meanwhile, there were two other besetting problems for Liza, the increasing dissension within the board of Wombles Ltd and the production of *Wombling Free*, a full-length film being produced by the actor-director Lionel Jeffries for the cinema. Her reaction to both problems were similar. Her old attitude of burying her head in the sand and hoping her problems would disappear had changed and she started to question other people's decisions. She had no business training but she was very principled when it came to money and could not understand, or believe, that others had a more elastic approach. The Womble 'pie' had grown and so, too, had those with fingers in it. Both Liza and Max believed that some of those fingers were sticky. Whether it was expenses being put through the company or percentages of different activities from licensing to overseas editions, Liza was never sure. 'Where does honesty begin let alone end?' she asked herself. Julian Lee, a family friend and highly successful city accountant, tried to explain the difference between tax avoidance and evasion to Liza:

Julian put for the most logical and obvious reasons tonight as to how we four directors should make the greatest (financial) use of profits, i.e. the best ways in which to avoid the greatest tax, e.g. one can charge a 'car allowance'. Perfectly legal, but that allowance has nothing whatever to do with using one's car on Womble business. You can charge this, that and the other legitimately, but it's none of it <u>true</u>. And when I say so, they say, 'Oh well it's the tax system and the government'. And they argue so well but to me, it's <u>cheating</u>.

'Do you want to live in Spencer Park?'

'Yes, I do.'

'Do you want to be independent when are old?'

'Yes, I do.'

'Do you want to leave a high percentage of your income to your children and not to the government?'

'Yes, I do.'

'Then there are measures you must take.'

Yes, yes, yes – I love my creature comforts. I love being dry, warm, food, drink, so am I prepared to give all that up in order to accept? This is where corruption starts. I am very lucky to be self indulgent but it does worry me, because none of it seems to be <u>right</u>. Pay unto Caesar that which is Caesar's – what does <u>that mean</u>? Pay to Caesar all that you are legally obliged to pay – fiddling as you go – but what about pay unto God? What about pay unto your country? What about pay unto your conscience? And conscience, as we know, is something you can only afford when you're well fed and warm.

Put into context, this was an era when basic income tax was 34 per cent, and at the top end 83 per cent, so every penny counted. It had been rumoured that the Wombles were a licence to print money, but they would have had to print an awful lot before anyone could make serious money. What Liza wanted, and I suspect a lot of children's writers must have also felt, was to please as many children as possible with a modicum of fuss.

As the 'suits' were all busy arguing about tax and percentages, Liza was seeing a very different picture out and about on her signings and library talks. At one library, Liza found herself talking to 100 children. A small boy started to cry:

I thought perhaps that he wanted to go to the loo or had wet his trousers. A librarian scooped him up and took him away – he cried again later. Afterwards the librarian told me he was a 7-year-old whose mother was on drugs ... they told me that when they went through a class of sixty-four, thirty-two were single parent families. In the borough hundreds of children roamed through the streets every night because the parents told them to get lost. But what can I *do*? I talk to them, I make them laugh and smile which is something, and being driven back tonight I saw those children everywhere, standing hand in hand on street corners and wanting to cross the road. Those ugly, ugly buildings and stretches of wasteland everywhere. How CAN those children grow even less than their parents? It's no good having a Doctor Barnardos outlook, to be a trendy-lefty, do-gooder attitude – I'll be good and kind to them and they will love me for it – something much more is needed – non-political, non-background.

The Borough Librarian, Mr MacNab, was lovely, large, a bit pompous and then straightforward nice. It was his staff who told me that he'd been on one of the Russian convoys (WW2), that he'd been one of the party who had scooped up a German submarine crew and that the officers all gave the Nazi salute. One school (present at the talk) gave me a beautiful book of drawings and stories. I do admire those teachers – they do such tremendous work against terrible odds – but nobody sings their praises.

And that smashing young man Trevor who drove me there and back today: he works and works at his job and after hours to help kids … and there's a big, burly 30 plus who really minds, and Mr MacNab and Trevor's wife Christine and Miss Wildman, the children's librarian. But nobody ever hears about people like them.

The other problem was the film *Wombling Free*, produced by Ian Shand and directed by Lionel Jefferies, which proved to be disappointing, through no fault of Liza's. It was another case of too many fingers in the pie. Lionel Jeffries had written the script and directed the film *The Railway Children*, based on the E. Nesbitt book which was a great success in 1970. Everyone expected that he would repeat his golden touch, but mixing humans and Wombles in a musical film was quite a different experience. This was in the days before CGI, so one of the first hurdles was to imagine how tall Wombles were compared with humans. Liza – somewhat randomly – said 4ft, and so small people were cast to play individual Wombles. With their costumes on, properly padded this time, they looked like very authentic Wombles but when they were placed alongside children, they somehow looked too large, even threatening.

From the start the script was doomed. Liza and David Wood, the actor and successful children's theatre writer, were the first scriptwriters as part of the agreement. Liza and David worked well together but behind the scenes there were moves to change things. On 7 March Liza recorded in her diary:

After some preliminaries David and I got down to working out a basic plot for the Pinewood film. It was an amalgam of ideas ... I would say that overall David and I contribute 50/50, i.e. it was my idea that the 'Womble super petrol' retrogressed into slow fuel. David backed this up by suggesting that ancient rubbish was needed for hi-speed [*sic*] fuel, newly processed rubbish produced only low-speed fuel. Before, over and after lunch, we produced a four-page treatment. After he'd gone I rang that terrifying woman Peggy Ramsay [theatrical agent] who scared me blue by saying it was a 'tremendously small budget', and that very little cash would be left over for writers' payments and that it must be a 'theatrical deal', i.e. that Rank [distributors] had to put the film on cinemas for five years before selling to TV, a very valid point.

Perhaps Liza and David had been thinking too 'small screen' for Lionel or Ian Shand, because a week later Lionel was on the phone to Liza:

He's certainly got a lot of lovely, heart-thumping ideas for the film, but I'm bad because when people are enthusiastic and gushing, I retire, like a hermit crab and all you see are the faint waverings of my claw ends ... Ramsay doesn't like the Pinewood set-up and was on the telephone for ONE hour.

By mid-March the pressure was on Liza. Ian Shand rang her to say he wanted:

David is out and me only to work to Lionel Jeffries, who will, I suspect, be the writer-director of the film AND they want to bring in Spike Milligan whom I feel will be all wrong so I was fighting on that front ... I know that Lionel is going to take over the scriptwriting of the film but he is an adaptor not a writer of plots. If the film is off-key it will damage the Wombles, Peggy Ramsay is on my side to protect the image!

Liza had FilmFair on her side, too. On 18 March she wrote:

> Graham Clutterbuck is off on Concorde tomorrow until the last week in April and has given me the power of veto on anything I don't like about the proposed film. So I'm in there fighting all on my own. I must learn to say <u>no</u> and not be afraid of hurting people's feelings.

She began work at Pinewood on 21 March and they finished the film scenes on 2nd April. There were funny moments. She was always worried about being late and one day she skittled through the set of the *New Avengers* without realising where she was until she heard 'cut!' and found herself face to face with Gareth Hunt, who played the character of Gambit; sportingly, he laughed his head off.

She never felt easy about the way the script was going, or working with Lionel. She liked him and he was very entertaining but she did not feel he understood her Wombles.

> Had my good driver today but he didn't hurry as he knew Lionel would be late. Arrived at Pinewood and there he [Lionel] was. Actors are unusual. He said he'd hated the whole of yesterday pm (BAFTA film awards) and then, of course, it transpired that he'd loved every minute. We stuck fast on the script for two hours and only gradually talked it out, but I'm not happy about the whole thing. It's not properly structured as a plot. We are being run so short of time and it's the old story of sinking the ship for a halfpenny of tar. Why this time? With a film it should be more serious. I'm not standing far enough back to get a proper look. It's got no shape. What I should do is write the whole story outline and then have it broken down into a shooting script. It must have a beginning, middle, end. There is no through plot, only a series of funny incidents. Lionel sees it all as a series of dramatic filmic pieces, I see it overall. It's not going to work except in a very minor way.

She was right. It was little more than a series of pastiches based on Mike Batt's Womble songs, re-scored for the film. In effect there were two stories, one about humans – Mr Frogmorton (David Tomlinson) who had a job in the City (reminiscent of Mary Poppins) and his wife Julia

(Frances de la Tour), their daughter Kim (Bonnie Langford) and their neighbours, a Japanese car dealer and his wife. Kim sees the Wombles because she believes in them and becomes their friend, and eventually even the father can see them and organises help for a great rubbish clear-up. In the meantime the Wombles invent a pollution-free car, stage a Hollywood musical extravaganza and launch the first-balloon-powered aircraft. The cast list makes interesting reading, however. Among the credits for the Womble voices were David Jason, Janet Brown, Bill Pertwee … and Lionel Jeffries. Liza was credited as Script Consultant.

There was talk – and some development work – of creating a Womble cartoon in America, masterminded by Al Broadax who had produced the final (and low budget) *Popeye* cartoons. In the end this came to nothing, but the books were sold to America as were ALL her romantic novels, which Liza was proud of and for which she was well remunerated. Her old horrors of being in debt had returned because the upgrade of the Alderney house, which was doubling in size, had cost far more than bargained for and she and Max were not selling their London house but keeping it on as a shared residence with paying guests, organised by me. The idea was that at some point in the future, they would return to pick up their Spencer Park lives once again.

At the beginning of 1978 Liza speculated about her future.

Financially I should do well with the burden of 22 [Little St] and Inland Revenue met at last. There go my life savings, but it will be an enormous weight off my shoulders if the house is paid off. It, the worry, has been like an albatross round my neck. My worry was that the money spent cancelled out the money saved and I, as blinkered as ever, couldn't see 22 as a capital asset. To me it is not a financial concern but a retreat. I also hated, and still do hate, the idea of leaving No 3 [Spencer Park] which is a beautiful house that I love very much. And I hate leaving all my friends and neighbours and the garden and the park. No 3 gives me enormous pleasure to look at and live in. One has to get used to the idea that one is only the momentary custodian of something that is grand and lovely in its own right, and also to realise that when one leaves it, it will no longer be the same place … when I go, I must go completely and without looking back. You have to take your own shell with you.

She was also worried – and rightly it turned out – that it would affect her marriage, thrown together with Max and nowhere in the house to escape from him. Sadly, by this time she had come to dislike him intensely: 'I don't trust him, don't like him and dread his return,' she wrote in January. In retrospect, it is extraordinary that they ever contemplated making a tiny island their home. Max had never enjoyed the Alderney life on his infrequent visits there. It was far too parochial for him, there was nowhere to go on antique jaunts and he loathed drinks parties, the beach and outdoor life, and felt little in common with the people he met. Liza had refused to contemplate living anywhere else if they had to leave London and Max's determination to beat the taxman was stronger than any doubts he had, so it was to the small Channel Island that they moved in March 1978.

The dissent within Wombles Ltd continued to rumble as they all pulled in different directions. Liza resented the interminable meetings more and more and as the day of her and Max's final move to Alderney approached, it was one of the few compensations that she could envisage: fewer board meetings.

March saw frantic preparations to sort through the house and offices before the great move. At the same time, the usual talks, interviews and book-signings went on and she was still writing, including a children's book for Methuen – *Toby's Luck* – and *Secret Magic* for Hart-Davis. But eventually the 'tryper' was packed away and the filing cabinets and her study 'vanished' as the removal men 'quickly spread like hungry, munching locusts through the house'. On Thursday, 30 March, on the orders of her old friend John Timpson, BBC's *Tonight* programme sent a camera crew to Wimbledon Common to film Liza's farewell to the home of the Wombles. Four rent-a-Wombles were in attendance. Liza wrote: 'It was amazing because the Common was empty but as soon as they appeared, children appeared – from behind bushes and trees with cries of "Wombles – it's the Wombles!" The Beeb crew were taken aback. We filmed and filmed over and over again.'

Once it was in the can she returned to Spencer Park for her last night there. She had cried for many a night at the thought of leaving the house, but there was no chance to catch her breath as various neighbours appeared to say goodbye; Marcus and I were there, too, and a roaring party was soon in progress.

The next morning Liza was driven by Marcus to Southampton Airport where the same camera crew were waiting to film her departure. The weather was wet and windy and Marcus remembers that he and Liza were filmed in the pouring rain getting into the tiny Trislander on the runway and sitting together. Then he disembarked and the cameraman took his seat instead and flew with Liza to Alderney. On 31 March 1978, Liza took up residence in her Alderney Burrow.

In true Liza fashion, the moment she set foot on Alderney as a 'settler' rather than 'holiday maker', she felt totally at home and cast any regrets at leaving London aside and dug herself into the fabric of the island and its community. It is one thing to have island holidays and quite another to live all year round on one, but she was a great adaptor and she began to relish what Alderney offered while Max very quickly realised his mistake.

It was not just his lack of conviviality that scuppered his chances of successful island living. There was no passenger ferry service to the other Channel Islands nor to the mainland, and the very efficient little sixteen-seater Trislander direct service to Southampton Airport and inter-islands was the only means of getting away. This was absolutely fine until flying was prevented because fog, or conversely very strong winds, made it impossible to fly, which was quite frequently – and somehow always at the most inconvenient moment. The airport could easily be closed for a few hours or even twenty-four hours, so any journeys had to be planned allowing a day either end 'just in case'. It was imperative therefore to have a relaxed attitude and an ability to cope with delay. Max might have been able to face this had he had the opportunity to leap into the car and drive off in search of antique shops, but that was not an option on terra firma measuring under four square miles.

It did not take long for No 22 Little Street to become a social hub for all manner of friends and acquaintances dropping in for a chat at the kitchen table, or a drink on the patio outside the kitchen door; anyone from the lighthouse keeper to the president could be found perched on bar stools at the kitchen counter. The new sitting room on the first floor, which faced south and flooded with light for much of the day with French windows opening onto the upper terrace, was made for parties. Max was happy to discuss antiques or wine with a select few, while Liza would pass round plate after plate of her famous cheese straws and chat to anyone about anything. In due course, they acquired a black-and-white stray kitten from the Impot (the island 'dump'), and named him Archie. He turned out to be a very characterful cat for whom even Max felt affection. Archie, who considered himself human, was very sociable and soon had all near neighbours under his spell. He was known to turn up at their drinks parties and enjoy himself thoroughly, hoovering up the canapés. Not surprisingly, he soon made an appearance in Liza's books too.

Journeys off-island were planned for maximum use of the shortest time and would incorporate promotional work, visiting family, or in Max's case, tennis commentary, most notably the Wimbledon fortnight. They were only allowed ninety days each on the UK mainland in order to remain within the tax rules, but after only three months of moving to Alderney, Liza was off to South Africa again for a book tour arranged by Puffin Books, publishers of *The Wombles* paperback editions. In East London, in the Cape, she opened the first Book Fair to be held in South Africa. Over the next ten years or so, Liza flew to California and several times to Kenya as the guest of Robin Hancox, their one-time lodger in Earlsfield Road, who had risen in the legal ranks to be the last British Chief Justice, based at Government House in Nairobi. Liza loved the country, especially down at the coast in Malindi and Watamu, where she swam every day in the deliciously warm Indian Ocean. Various friends accompanied her, including Shirley Berkeley-Smith, always excellent company with her quick and amusing wit, and Jenny Gosney, a very talented cook (a tester for Mary Berry no less) and a fount of theatrical and showbiz knowledge. Her youngest brother, the theatre designer Tony Walton, was Julie Andrews's first husband. Julie very kindly let Jenny and Liza use her Gstaad chalet for a holiday one year and Jenny made a delicious fish pie which she put in the state-of-the-art, eye-level oven and turned it on to cook while they went out for a bracing walk. On their return, Liza and Jen, ravenous and looking forward to a glass of wine or two with the fish pie, discovered that unfortunately Jenny had turned the oven to self-clean, not cook. The fish pie had more or less evaporated into a black cinder.

A year after the move to Alderney, Margaret Thatcher led the Conservatives into government and in their first budget the top rate of tax was reduced from 83 per cent to 60 per cent, but there was no return to the UK for Liza and Max; the die was cast. Coincidentally, the Womble income had dropped off considerably and Liza was back at her 'tryper' yet again and her night-time devils were never far away when the black cloud of Mr Micawber's prediction: 'Annual income twenty pounds, annual expenditure twenty pounds nought and six, result misery' would linger at the front of her mind. It was hoped that her new book, *The Tovers*, would prove to be a bestseller. *The Tovers* were a product of her love of gardening – fairy-like creatures which were a hybrid of *Borrowers* and *Hobbits* (she had read neither Mary Norton nor J.R.R. Tolkien) – which was a lively and inventive read, but sold only moderately.

Liza's imagination and compulsion to write was ignited by the possibilities that Alderney offered, not only as material for her books but also the local talent on the island with whom she collaborated. Some of the most enjoyable and funny moments arose from her collaboration with Ronnie Cairnduff, a filmmaker who spent several months of each year on the island. They were both involved in 'Alderney Week', a week in August comprising all sorts of events from the barmy Man-powered Flight to the Cavalcade, culminating in a bonfire and fireworks. Regular tourists came back every year to take part and indeed they still do, now bringing their grandchildren to enjoy the week of wonderful celebration of island life. In a bid to prolong the fun, Liza and Ronnie were sitting in the kitchen at No 22, thinking how nice it would be to do something different.

Gradually the idea for a film took shape: it would be silent so that no one had to learn lines, and made in black and white so that Ronnie would not have to worry about lighting. 'Liza quickly got the idea of *Rosebud the Girl From Casquets*,' Ronnie remembers. The Casquets is a group of rocks, north-west of Alderney, hazardous to shipping and totally uninhabitable, but offered an air of mystery. They chose the locations on Alderney, including the stretch of single-track rail from the harbour to the quarry at the other end of the island along which ran two ex-Bakerloo Line carriages from the London Underground. Ronnie brought a small crew over from the mainland.

'It was hilarious to make,' he recalls. 'We had huge assistance from the police who closed off the roads and when word got about everyone wanted to be in it.' Maggie Cranwell, a talented young friend of Liza's who at the time was teaching at the island school, was cast as Rosebud and, well known for her quick wit and loquaciousness, was soon in character as an eyelash-batting, damsel in distress who never stopped talking but of course could not be heard. At one point, Maggie was tied to the railway line in a nod to Charlie Chaplin films which Liza had loved as a child. 'The railway came under the auspices of British Rail and we had to have a licence,' Ronnie remembers. 'I told them that there would be about 100yards between Maggie and the stopped train. In the event, the driver took rather longer to stop and the panic in his eyes was not faked!' Professional that Maggie was, she just kept batting her eye lashes. The finished film had its premiere on the island and was reported in a double-page spread in the Nigel Dempster column of the *Daily Mail!* There was an immediate clamour for more *Rosebud* and two further films were made.

In all three films the villain – Sir Arlott Johns – was played by the retired, larger-than-life cricket commentator John Arlott, who enjoyed himself enormously. I remember acting as his henchwoman in the second film, *Rosebud and the Godfathers*, and having to row John ashore with the tide against me, as he threw empty brandy bottles past my ears into the sea as required by Liza's script. The film crew – including Liza – nearly killed themselves laughing while I nearly killed myself trying to battle against the odds with a heavyweight national treasure in the stern. On another occasion he was supposed to knock back a glass of wine laced with 'poison'. Props had supplied cheap plonk and John, who was a wine connoisseur, took one swig and spat it out in disgust in the manner of Captain Haddock drinking water. 'I can't drink this muck!' he said. He drove home and then reappeared with four bottles of his best claret.

In the third and final film, *Murder on the Alderney Express,* Liza had a Hitchcock moment and cast herself as a passenger on the train. She was far too good and upstaged everyone. 'We worked well together,' Ronnie recalls. 'Liza would come up with the ideas and I would facilitate them. We had endless evenings in her kitchen, drinking wine and laughing. It was a great, great time.'

In addition to the films, Liza also wrote the book and lyrics for several island musicals in conjunction with Betty Cherrett, who composed the music. These were based on Alderney themes such as *The Little Mermaid* and *God Save the Queen*, which was about Queen Victoria's visit to the island in the nineteenth century, and packed the Island Hall for several performances. The cast took a lot of rehearsing and in the time-honoured way of many directors of amateur productions, Liza was driven mad by the lack of professional commitment among some members of the cast, but somehow they all came together in the end and the show went on.

Another fertile island collaboration was with Jane Aireton, a former nurse, who had come up with the idea of a children's character called *Bertie the Bat*. With Liza writing the scripts based on Jane's ideas and drawings, they put together a pilot for Channel Television. It was accepted and ten very charming five-minute episodes were recorded and transmitted in 1991. The voices were all recorded by Bernard Cribbins.

The quality of life on the island for Liza was much calmer than her earlier, frenetic life. Gone were the days of driving through London and beyond; on the island an average journey was about a mile. There was no MOT and she had a succession of beaten-up motors which had to have their batteries on constant charge and were almost impossible to start in the winter. One, an old Morris 1100 nicknamed 'The Colonel', was so rusty – sea salt in the air was a constant problem – that in the passenger seat you could see the cobbled road trundling by beneath your feet.

In the spring, Liza was like Mole in *Wind in the Willows*, lifting her face to the sky, sniffing the sea and feeling the warmer sun, which put a skip in her tread. She loved the much smaller and more manageable garden where she planted out vegetables and tomatoes in the greenhouse and once the summer arrived, she swam when she could, went to al fresco art classes, and even joined the railway rota as a station master. There were always parties, including delicious lunches with near neighbours Peter and Isabelle Bowen when they were over on the island. Peter was a wine importer and many an excellent bottle was quaffed in the company of friends. Liza became 'honorary Granny' to their three children.

Liza also took her civic duty seriously and for three years was an elected member of the States of Alderney, one of the world's oldest parliaments and whose origins are lost in the mists of time. Alderney had originally belonged to Normandy but, with the other Channel Islands, became part of William the Conqueror's realm. Today it is a self-governing Crown Dependency within the Bailiwick of Guernsey. The ten elected councillors and the president are responsible for overseeing the various public services of the island, much like a town council would on the mainland. Naturally, it is run by committees which was anathema to Liza, who was constantly trying to 'get things done' outside committee meetings. She stood for one term and that was it, she had had enough of what she thought of as 'too much waffle and not enough action'. She went on using the vast quantity of briefing papers as scrap for jotting down story ideas, lists and messages for the rest of her life.

She much preferred putting her energies into helping with the tiny prep school on the island, Ormer House. This was run by Maggie Cranwell of *Rosebud* fame, now married to one of the Aurigny pilots, Ralph Burridge. The school, with fewer than 20 pupils, gave an excellent all-round education for boys and girls aged 3 to 12 and was accepted as a 'feeder' school for mainland public schools. It meant that parents wishing to educate their children privately did not have to send them away to the mainland, and the form sizes were so small the pupils received wonderfully dedicated teaching. Liza, perhaps remembering the dame school she was sent to during the war, supported Maggie and the school as best she could. 'She was a Governor, Trustee and all round good egg,' Maggie recalls.

Liza continued working and writing children's books. The last Wombles book – *Wombling Free* – was published in 1978. There were three more 'magic' books, *Secret Magic* (Hart-Davis 1978), *Curious Magic* (Granada 1980) and *Strange Magic* (Methuen 1986), twenty-two other children's titles, including one based on her experiences as a child called *Lizzie's War* (Simon & Schuster 1993), which sold very well and was used in schools to explain what it was like to be an evacuee in wartime. She also wrote a further five romantic novels, often peopled with real island characters (who luckily did not recognise themselves).

There were two enormous upheavals which nearly brought her little piece of heaven crashing down about her ears, causing her heartache and despair. The first was the deterioration of her marriage to Max. She confessed that she had begun to hate him and felt a physical dislike of his presence. The age difference of eleven years was increasingly obvious and she thought of him as an old man as he approached his 70th birthday. What Max did not know was that Liza had been having an affair for several years with a slightly younger, married man. He had no idea until he did the one thing that no one should ever do without asking permission – he read her diary. One can only feel sorry for him, although he had countless affairs during their marriage, when he read about her passion for another man. His pride was dealt a deep, irreparable blow and unbeknown to Liza, he set about arranging his departure from the island, from her and from their marriage. But before he left, there was one last familial duty he had to perform.

Marcus, now aged 28, had met and become engaged to the beautiful and clever Marianne Rivaz, whose parents had also retired to the island. Their wedding was set for 28 September 1984, the day after Max and Liza's 35th wedding anniversary. Friends and relatives flew in from the mainland, the weather was warm and sunny and the wedding at St Anne's church was a very happy one. Everyone enjoyed themselves at the reception, held at a hotel on Braye Beach. The following day, Sunday, Marcus and Marianne flew off on their honeymoon, guests and family returned to the mainland. On Monday, Liza got the shock of her life when a removals lorry turned up and Max announced that he 'knew all' and was moving to Guernsey. He did not behave well; rather, he wanted her to pay him £75,000 or he would spill the beans and her name would be mud on the island and her lover's family would be deeply hurt. Liza called it blackmail, but she paid – 'there go my life savings' she wrote despairingly in her diary. He said he had taken 'photostats', and for some years thereafter she lived in dread that he would use them against her.

Max flew off that same day and they did not meet again for over ten years. They did, however, continue to write to one another quite affectionately and speak often on the telephone. To begin with Liza felt terrible guilt and wondered whether she should follow him to Guernsey as she knew he would be incapable of looking after himself. In a diary entry for 11 July 1989, she wrote: 'Max was a dreadful bully but if I'd stood up to him he would probably have been a great deal happier.' Quite soon she became more pragmatic, and then began to realise that life was simpler without him.

The other body blow Liza suffered was the Lloyds of London crash in the late 1980s–early1990s. When she and Max had moved to the island they became friends with a number of tax exiles who had become 'Names' at Lloyds. Where once investors had to show vast wealth to become a Name, by the late 1970s applications were welcome from individuals with liquid assets of £250,000. Join the right syndicate, they said, and you will get an excellent return on your investment. Liza was encouraged to become a Member and she was elected on 21 December 1979. All went well for the first few years until two disasters hit the market (hard on the heels of a scandal about sharp practice in Lloyds): historical asbestos claims and the Piper Alpha disaster in 1988. The oil rig exploded in the North Sea causing loss of life and a £1.4bn loss for Lloyds, which the Names had to meet. It was discovered that risks had been reinsured many times over and some syndicates – including the one Liza was in – were very badly hit by multiple claims. Until then, most individuals who had been elected to Lloyds had never understood that they had committed to unlimited liability, namely they could be forced into bankruptcy. Liza's wealth, such as it was, disappeared into the miasma and misery of Lloyds, and if it had not been for the brilliant advice and know-how of Marcus, who by this time was running his own sports agency and was extremely hard-working and acute, she would have lost her beloved house. The old spectre of the bailiffs came back to haunt her and she immediately set about getting extra work, including cleaning and answering the telephone at a friend's offices in the town.

Then a chink of light lit up her tunnel of doom as Great Uncle Bulgaria and the Wombles came unexpectedly to the rescue.

Chapter 9

Wombles to the Rescue

The Womble television films were often repeated over the years by the BBC until their option ran out in 1989, so the Wombles were still scrabbling away just below the surface of national consciousness. The films were shown overseas, too, and on one of her visits to Kenya, Liza reported seeing them on television in Nairobi. In 1987 FilmFair was acquired by Central Television, and Graham Clutterbuck wrote to Liza in August that year to say: 'We are now interested in redeveloping *The Wombles* ... Mike Batt is extremely keen on relaunching the Wombles musically, based on a new television series.' Mike and Graham were talking about a new type of animation – cartoons – that they could sell into the American market. However, Graham died within a few months of this discussion and Lewis Rudd, head of children's programming at ITV Central (1981–94), took over as the new Chairman of FilmFair. Much to Liza's delight he supported a relaunch of the stop-frame Wombles and one of the first things he did was to authorise the re-run of some of the original Womble episodes during the autumn and run-up to Christmas. He also commissioned two half-hour specials: *The Wandering Wombles* and *World Womble Day*. Liza wrote the scripts and faxed them over from her kitchen counter to David Yates, Director of Production at FilmFair, and once again Bernard Cribbins supplied the voices.

Some of the original puppets had disappeared or were damaged and had to be recreated, new sets were made and extra characters introduced to try and broaden the Wombles' international appeal. In *World Womble Day*, long before Zoom calls, the worldwide Wombles were communicating by homemade Wellicom (invented by Wellington), planning a 300th birthday for Great Uncle Bulgaria: new Wombles included Cairngorm MacWomble the Terrible, a rather short-tempered Scottish Womble who had appeared in the books but not the early films and was based on Max; Serengeti Womble in East Africa, Woy-Woy in Australia, and Obidos in

South America. Environmental problems were increasing and had moved up the agenda since the 1970s. Even the rubbish had to be updated to include Styrofoam packaging, satellite dishes, old calculators and other bits of electronic detritus.

Word got out that the Wombles were coming back and even the Government lobbied Liza for help. Replying to Virginia Bottomley, Parliamentary Under-Secretary of State for the Environment, after a meeting in the spring of 1989, Liza wrote to her:

> There are hopes of a thirty-minute Womble 'special' which will be shown just before Christmas 1990. It will give me <u>great</u> pleasure to write a few succinct remarks for Great Uncle Bulgaria on the question of the environment and Human Beings in particular. <u>He</u> started talking along these lines in 1969 ... So if there is anything they can do to help children 'Womble up the rubbish' or 'make good use of bad rubbish', they would be delighted.

The relaunch was a tremendous opportunity to kickstart merchandising and the possibility of a much needed income stream for Liza. FilmFair's Licensing Director, Jane Evans, issued a press release to the merchandising media in which she said:

> Although the BBC continued to air the Wombles series, the ITV network gave them a higher profile and better slots. At the same time, FilmFair which had recently been taken over by Central, felt that the Wombles had the strongest potential from the properties in our archives and deserved to be successful. We did research at various places around the country and there was enormous affection towards the characters. What we agreed with Elisabeth was that this time around we would be seeking to achieve a more gradual expansion of licences.

One of the most important developments in all this was that Walker Books took up the publishing rights, which had lapsed as Ernest Benn had become defunct. They reissued the novels in paperback, with new and very charming illustrations by Edgar Hodges, and the books were in the Children's Top Ten Bestseller list in no time at all. Liza was delighted and so was her bank manager. In 1991 they reissued the Womble picture books with new illustrations, again by Edward Hodges.

Gradually, the awful pressures of paying Lloyds bills were released. Marcus ensured that Liza joined Equitas, a group of companies that was formed by Lloyds in 1996 to assume, via reinsurance, the enormous and crippling liabilities that had accumulated in the Lloyds syndicates. Equitas, the Wombles merchandising money and publishing royalties meant that Liza was once again in the black. On 10 May 1997, she wrote:

> Marcus said today I could be out of the Lloyd's killing fields. It has been such a long and deadly tunnel and I have had to crawl and crawl and probably will have to again. Every time in life you get up onto your knees you get slapped round the ears and your face pushed into the slime. It doesn't matter. What matters is making life a millimetre better for the next generation.

Children always fascinated Liza, especially how they saw the world. It was therefore especially wonderful that she became a grandmother when Marcus and Marianne produced two sons, Charlie and Ben, born two years apart on the same day in 1988 and 1990. Although they lived in Surrey, they had bought a holiday home a few doors down from Liza's house so she saw the boys several times every year. Naturally, both boys were written into her books.

During this time, approaching the age of 70, Liza's imagination was still at full throttle. She invented a new cast of characters for Channel TV. The cartoon *Dawdle and the Donkey* ran for three series from 1996 to 1998 with a total of thirty-three episodes. The premise was that Dawdle was lost in the city, looking for somewhere to live. She meets Rola Pola Bear and Archie the Cat, who are also homeless, and they decide to find a place to share. Eventually they make their way to the countryside and Dawdle sees a glowing Golden Gate. Dawdle believes that the glow means it is an entrance to a magic meadow and persuades her friends to make their home there, and so their adventures begin. Dawdle was voiced by Josie Lawrence and Rola Pola Bear by David Jason. The theme song was sung by Chris de Burgh. The cartoons can still be seen on YouTube.

In January 1992, The Storm Group acquired FilmFair from Central TV and then in 1996, the Montreal-based company Cinar entered the picture, when they bought the FilmFair archive. What began then was Liza's last collaboration with the Wombles on television. Cinar commissioned fifty-two episodes over four series and each episode ten minutes in length, twice the original length. This was not the only change: they were to be voiced by Canadian actors, not by Bernard Cribbins, despite vociferous lobbying by Liza; and new 'politically correct' characters were introduced, including Stepney, who was given darker fur and dreadlocks by the designers.

This was very much against Liza's wishes, because to her the Wombles were all the same wherever they lived in the world, they all had grey fur with slightly orange faces and paws as designed by Ivor Wood. She never discriminated, and argued that by introducing a character with black fur it immediately set it apart from the others. However, North America was already in the grip of political correctness which has proved to be so destructive and the Canadians were adamant. Stepney was joined by Shansi, an expert gardener from China who was made to look Oriental. Alderney, who had made a brief appearance in the novels, was another new Womble whose feisty character was based on Marcus's wife Marianne. She did not live in the burrow but in the tree above and was something of an eco-warrior concerned about water pollution. Cairngorm MacWomble the Terrible returned, joined by Obidos from South America, Moosonee from the Rocky Mountains and various other bit-part Wombles.

Liza wrote the scripts and faxed them to me for editing and suggestions and then I sent them on to FilmFair, now in North London, for production and filming. The Canadian voices were dubbed in Canada. At first they were too frenetic and characterless, far removed from the brilliance of Bernard. They quietened down, but remained rather like Dick Van Dyke's famed rendition of the cockney chimneysweep, Bert, in *Mary Poppins*. They were barely recognisable as the original members of Liza's family on which they were based. The series was shown from 5 March 1997 to 10 April 2000.

By 1998, Liza's health had begun to be of concern. Not surprisingly, after all the worries of Lloyds and pressure of work, her heart and her hip were beginning to worry her. However, nothing was going to stop her from going to Buckingham Palace to receive her MBE from the Queen. She was notified in November 1997 that she had been awarded the honour for her contribution to children's literature and community work in Alderney. Marcus waggishly renamed the honour as Mother's Best Effort. She wrote in her diary: 'Who me? Oh wouldn't Ma be pleased – I'm so glad for her – don't think Daddy would think much of it – he was rather anti-Establishment … Kate and Marcus are pleased – we have agreed to keep it quiet from Max – all his BBC contemporaries seem to have got something – it's tricky.'

Liza was right, Trissie would have been extremely proud, fervent royalist that she was. The day her eldest son, Tristram, collected his CBE at the Palace he was ordered to report straight back to her with no detail to be held back. Liza was a great believer in the monarchy as well and for many years gave what was known on the island as the 'other queen's speech'. This was a story she would make up and tell to local children, filmed by Channel TV and transmitted on Christmas Eve.

Liza flew over to Southampton on Monday, 16 February 1998. She did not know it then, but it was to be her last visit to London and the mainland. She stayed with me where I lived in Earlsfield, and the moment she arrived the press calls started coming in. The very next morning a BBC van was parked outside my house to the bemusement of neighbours, and Liza clambered into the back where she did a piece for Radio 5. I then drove her to Wimbledon Common where Marcus, Marianne, Charlie and Ben were waiting along with TV, radio and the press, as well as three rent-a-Wombles, Orinoco, Great Uncle Bulgaria and Alderney. It was a magic moment seeing them amble across the common to greet their creator. That night we watched ourselves on BBC and ITV News with a feeling of excited apprehension about what the next day was to bring.

The following morning Marcus drove us plus a family friend, Edward Bowen (who had started the petition for her MBE), to Buckingham Palace. Liza recorded the day in her diary:

We lined up in the car queue outside the palace – wonderful watching other people – into the front forecourt and then we were parted once inside. I had to climb a scarlet-carpeted, long staircase – great paintings everywhere – into the Picture Gallery. I was glad to sit down. A lot of elderly, anxious WRVS women – one tiny woman came and perched by me, she turned out to be Inland Revenue! The staff were all so smiling and friendly. The young girl who put the 'hook' on my coat had only left university last year and <u>loved</u> her work. Smattering of service men – like a drinks party without the drinks. A Gentleman Usher gave us all our instructions. At 11 it all began in the ballroom and we could all watch it on three screens. I was handing out peppermints to lovely Gurkhas by this time. We were called and we walked through the ballroom to a side apartment and lined up again. I talked to a lovely RAF man from the Isle of Man. And then suddenly you're ON. We'd all been very well drilled and HM was smiling at me and said something like 'I want to thank you for all you've done'. She knew about the Wombles and chatted quite a bit. One has seen her so often it is curiously like meeting an old friend. Curtsied and off, cornered instantly by the Press Association.

Watching the ceremony, Marcus and I were very moved and proud of our mother. As the Queen pinned the MBE to Liza's dress, it was a moment when two Elizabeths, both born in 1926, showed their respect for one another. The following morning I drove Liza to Broadcasting House where she was interviewed by Jenni Murray for *Woman's Hour*. 'Chatted on as usual – so strange being back in studio B13,' she observed. The following day, much to her huge relief, Marcus took her to Southampton and she was off back to her beloved Alderney, her heart beating in double time.

That last visit to London marked, in a way, Liza's farewell to her old life. Her heart trouble was diagnosed as arrhythmia and she had to take life at a gentler pace. She got tired easily and gave up drinking alcohol. That summer she was admitted first to the island cottage hospital, The Mignot, and then, fearful that she was going to have a full-blown heart attack, she was flown as an emergency to the hospital in Guernsey where facilities were far more sophisticated. Having been told to expect the worst, Marcus and I flew out to Guernsey where they very kindly extended the permitted landing time and kept the airfield lights on. Screeching up to the hospital with our own hearts in our mouths, we rushed to her hospital bedside hoping we were not too late. We need not have worried. She was sitting up in bed and said, 'What are you doing here?' She recovered well but it took the stuffing out of her. Then in October, she was considered well enough to have her bad hip replaced. This, too, went well and she enjoyed a week of rest, recuperation and physiotherapy, charming the hospital staff and visited by, among others, Max.

She returned to Alderney but two days later the new hip dislocated and she was medevacked once more to Guernsey in considerable pain. The hip was put back in place and it never bothered her again, but she had lost all her confidence and never regained her old bounce. To begin with she managed on her own, with cleaning help. She would sit with her 'tryper' at the end of the kitchen table, answering fan mail, writing the odd article and, of course, entertaining anyone who came through the red front door, usually without knocking. In the summer, the Island Tour bus would stop outside the house and visitors would gawp while Liza chuckled to herself. For a few years she took in two lodgers, Terry and Russ, Aurigny pilots who were rarely there at the same time as each other, so she had a comforting male presence in the house. They were both very kind and thoughtful and she adored them, but when they reached the age of 60 they had to retire from the airline, first Terry and then Russ. She also had a succession of (mostly) kind and practical South African carers who laughed at her jokes and cherished her.

After a lengthy stay in the Mignot Memorial Hospital where she received wonderful care, Liza died late on Christmas Eve 2010, thirteen months after Max. Her Christian faith was very important to her, she believed implicitly in her guardian angel, so the Eve of the Nativity was a perfect day on which to die. Her ashes reside in the memorial garden beside St Anne's church, but I strongly suspect that her spiritual home is the South Downs above Brighton where she lies on her back, listening to the rippling grass and the cries of birds wheeling above her, looking at the blue, blue sky and dreaming of...

Afterword

In 2022 the word 'journey' is overused, as are 'passion' and the ubiquitous question 'how do you feel?' And normally I would be loathe to use them, but not on this occasion. Reading though my mother's diaries and letters has been, to say the least, an eye-opener and quite a journey, reliving her life and mine to a certain extent. I felt emotionally and physically exhausted inhabiting Liza's skin and as a result I am more passionate than ever about her legacy, her children's books and the Wombles and what they have meant to the world. Just before she died, Bloomsbury Books reissued the original novels, illustrated by Nick Price, with which she was delighted. She felt that whatever reincarnation the Wombles took in the future, her books were secure. The written word, the stories she told about the Wombles of Wimbledon Common, based on her family members, is the original creation of a unique imagination which Ivor and Bernard brilliantly brought to life in the Womble animations.

Of course it is not only her children's books and the animated films that are her legacy. Three generations have passed since *The Wombles* made their first appearance and with every passing year, there has grown a greater understanding and knowledge of the environment in which we live. The Wombles have been adopted by countless litter-picking groups, not only in this country but around the world. Close to home, in my own village, there is a group called The Womblings and, weather permitting, we go out once a week. More rubbish than ever is being thrown out of cars and lorries, regardless of the harm it does to wildlife and the environment, making more work for Wombles. I have seen corporation dust carts with Wombles in their cab windows because the bin crews are proud to be clearing rubbish and making a better environment for all. AFC Wimbledon have their own Womble mascot, Haydon, sanctioned by Liza, and when they returned to their new stadium in Plough Lane, they erected an Orinoco Womble bench and held a litter-pick among the local community.

Some communities also adopt Wombles for their recycling ideas and try to extend the life of objects that are thrown away without a second thought.

Liza was way ahead of the curve when she created the Wombles. Her experiences in the war – being bombed out of her home, living with rations, and having to 'make do and mend' – live on in *The Wombles*. When she did make money she did not really know what to do with it. Books and wine for her friends were her only two luxuries so she gave money to the church, to the Alderney Youth Group, to children's charities, and she 'fostered' children in the Third World.

It was always her greatest desire to make children laugh and to make them feel safe. 'As long as I can make them laugh,' was her constant refrain. This was what she did. What more can one ask?

Acknowledgements

The source material used in this book is primarily my mother's diaries. She would fill a page of an A5 diary nearly every day, sometimes catching up a week or so later. If the sequence of events is a bit hazy every now and then it is because there was usually no way of double-checking what she recorded in the diaries. For instance, she always used to say that the seminal visit to Wimbledon Common was on Boxing Day, but her diary records it as a few days before Christmas. It's a far better story to say Boxing Day and that is what I remember it as being ... but was it? If you are told something enough times, the truth can differ, even if you were there! Where possible I have checked through her letters to the family. She was an assiduous letter writer and I would receive at least one letter a week when I was away at boarding school and then university.

Most of the photographs in this book have come from private family albums, specifically Liza's and mine. However, some have been purchased and credited as such. There maybe a few photographs which were taken by professional photographers decades ago whom I have attempted to trace but without success.

This book is not to be a definitive history of Elisabeth Beresford and her writing, rather it is a fond memoir of a mother who also happened to be the creator of the Wombles. Anyone interested in delving further into her work for research or analysis will find her papers of interest which have been deposited at Seven Stories, the National Centre for Children's Books in Newcastle.

My thanks are nearer to home. First to my family, brother Marcus and his wife Marianne for their recollections and help with the Lloyds Fiasco. Also to the late great Bernard Cribbins who shared his recollections with me not long before he died; Jenny Gosney, a great friend of Bernard and Liza, who shared her memories; as did Maggie Burridge, who has been a friend of the family since the mid-1960s, and one of the funniest people

I know; Ronnie Cairnduff, director of the *Rosebud* films, and long-time collaborator with Liza in Alderney; Isabelle Bowen and her daughter Emma, who now live on Alderney, who, with Isabelle's late husband Peter and other children Arabella and Edward, were neighbours and friends of Liza's; Annie Tavener (née Buckmaster), a great schoolfriend of mine and secretary to Max and Liza in the formative Womble years; Josianne Wood, Ivor Wood's widow, who was the bookkeeper at FilmFair and checked my facts; Barry Leith, who was also a brilliant puppet maker at FilmFair and recalls thrashing out the scripts with Liza; Tom Sanders, an animator whose blog *The World of Ivor Wood*, makes great reading and who shared his photographs; Tara Stockford, whose Tidybag website is dedicated to all things Womble and who suggested to the publishers that I should write this book; AFC Wimbledon, now back in their rightful home at Plough Lane, for establishing an Orinoco Womble wooden seat outside the ground and keeping the Womble flame burning inside the stadium; my cousins Penny Joppe and Gill Gould who keep their Aunt Liza's creations in the public consciousness; Alan Strutt, photographer, for his help; Andrea Davies, who has kept my garden going and made me laugh when the going has been tough.

I would also like to thank the publishers Pen & Sword, especially Charlotte Mitchell who has tolerated my lateness and helped me keep focused, and Karyn Burnham for her forensic and professional editing.

Finally, to my long-suffering friends in London and Rudgwick, thank you all so much for your understanding, tolerance and amazing friendship, especially The Fletcher Food Fund, the Birthday Girls and The Old Stagers. You all know who you are!

Kate Robertson
November 2022

Index